AF470628

SURREY CCC
On This Day

SURREY CCC
On This Day

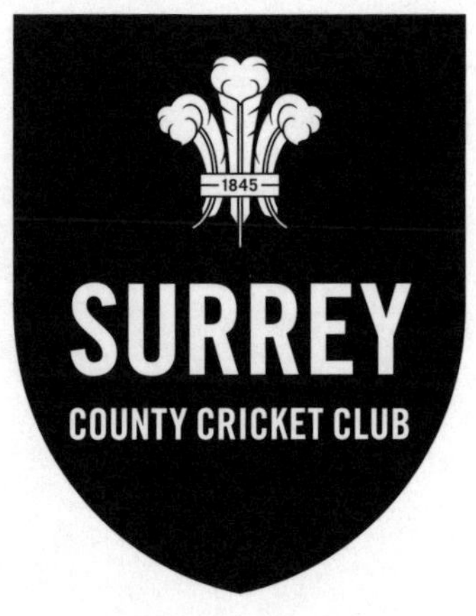

*History, Facts & Figures
from Every Day of the Year*

JON SURTEES

SURREY CCC
On This Day

History, Facts & Figures from Every Day of the Year

Published By:
Pitch Publishing (Brighton) Ltd
A2 Yeoman Gate
Yeoman Way
Durrington
BN13 3QZ

Email: info@pitchpublishing.co.uk
Web: www.pitchpublishing.co.uk

Published 2013

ISBN 9781909178533

Typesetting and origination by Pitch Publishing.
Printed in Great Britain by CPI Group.

FOREWORD

Surrey County Cricket Club and The Oval are as rich in cricketing history as it is possible to be.

Ever since the club was founded in 1845, its players have been involved at every stage of cricketing history as the sport has travelled around the world. Closer to home, our ground has hosted just about all the great cricketers who have played the game.

It is an honour and a privilege for me to have represented Surrey CCC and the content of this book underlines the stature and history of the club.

True legends of the game like Sir Jack Hobbs, Sir Alec Bedser, Peter May, Tom Hayward, Andy Sandham and John Edrich who have played for Surrey CCC should always be an inspiration for all of our current and future players.

This club has been a huge part of our family for well over 60 years. My father Micky made his first-class debut in 1954 and has maintained a very close association ever since as a player, captain, manager and president so I guess it was only natural that my affection for Surrey since signing as a professional in 1981 is just as strong today as it was then.

As a Surrey player I am very proud to have been a part of a squad that won a full house of trophies available but reading through the events described here it became even clearer to me that these trophies were the continuation of a long and proud history.

There has always been an expectation of success at Surrey and I hope that the winning of trophies and providing England with players from the club is a never-ending story.

On every page of this book you will read about players living up to this expectation. Whether it is a seemingly everyday piece of brilliance by the likes of Jim Laker, Tony Lock or Mark Ramprakash, or a less well known player elevating himself to their level, these are the players that have continued this tradition for over 140 years.

Whenever I meet Surrey fans across the world, I am often asked who the very best Surrey player I played with was. As you can imagine, this is a virtually impossible question to answer given the number of high quality players to have represented the club during my time. Graham Thorpe, Mark Ramprakash, Martin Bicknell, Waqar Younis, Sylvester Clarke and

Saqlain Mushtaq all spring to mind but I will leave it to you to help make my choice!

While I still can't single out one player, I have relived some fantastic memories through these pages. Entries for 12 July, 2 September and 13 September bring back some fantastic memories, as do 24 February, 12 April and 8 September.

Many people are immensely proud of Surrey County Cricket Club – for a very good reason. I hope you enjoy reading this book and finding out exactly why.

Alec Stewart

ACKNOWLEDGEMENTS

The first person I need to thank is the man without whom none of this book would have been written. He paid for my first ticket, bowled to me for hours as I gleefully smashed tennis balls into an old people's home and the sides of his neighbours' cars and also spent a great deal of time proof -reading this book. For all of this I am hugely thankful and his enthusiasm for life is always an inspiration. Dad, thanks very much.

Naturally I also need to thank 'The Gaffer', Alec Stewart, for agreeing to write the foreword to this book. I am very lucky that through the course of the last ten years I have been able to meet a large number of people that were heroes to me in a younger life. None have been as generous with their time, knowledge and experience as 'Stewie' and it still slightly freaks me out that I can call him a mate.

A very important thank you I would like to add is to every cricket statistician, scorer and historian that has ever spent time recording the game – and their modern counterparts who have spent time digitising it to make it so readily accessible. They are easily – and unfairly – mocked but their passion for what they do is a shining example.

Particular personal thanks should go to Jerry Lodge and Richard Spiller for their help and advice on this book – and also to Jo Miller, whose meticulous organisation of the Surrey Archive has made this project far easier than it might otherwise have been.

Finally, and most importantly, I need to thank Rachel. Unusually, there is nothing specific I can think of to thank her for, so I will have to settle for thanking her for everything.

INTRODUCTION

Ever since I was taken to Lord's as a wide-eyed six-year-old to watch the West Indies terrify the life out of England in the late 1980s, the sport of cricket has held a very special place in my heart.

My continuing affection for the game though is despite its often laughable anachronisms and elitist affectations. Given half a chance, I would far rather be on the bank at Newlands, by the bar at the Kensington Oval or in the shadow of the fort at Galle than corpulently slumped on a bench in St John's Wood as my garishly adorned boater is buffeted by the post-lunch snoring of those around me.

If this school of thought has a home then surely it's The Oval? England's oldest Test ground has seen them all over the years and still retained a refreshingly unpretentious air.

Part of the reason for that is the ground's position not just as a venue for grand occasions but as the home of a constantly functioning county club. The history of The Oval and the history of Surrey CCC are linked as one and I hope that has been reflected in this book.

From Montpelier CC and the dinners at the Horns Tavern through glorious periods in the 1890s, 1950s and the turn of the 20th century, Surrey CCC has been an integral part of British sport since long before the invention of the car.

Not satisfied with giving the world the likes of Tom Richardson, Sir Jack Hobbs, Alec Bedser, Jim Laker, Peter May, Graham Thorpe and Alec Stewart, Surrey can also lay claim to the legacy of the FA Cup, international football and rugby union.

Put simply, the history of Surrey CCC is the history of cricket. The stories in this book cover every country to have played the game and every last one of the game's greatest players has been tested beneath the Kennington gasholders.

This book barely scratches the surface of the incredible history of this great club. While I have tried hard to include as much as I can, I will inevitably have left out some people's golden memories. For this I apologise but I still hope you have enjoyed the rest!

Before researching this book I had no idea how wide a web of connections is held by the club. Read on and you will find links to Olympic gold medals, supersonic flight, Oscar-winning films, great British generals, internationally renowned rock stars, the Royal family, international politics at the highest level – and a friendly labrador called Bumper who just wanted to play!

Whether you pick up this book as a knowledgeable member, curious fan or, frighteningly, as a reference tool, I hope it gives you what you want and you are able to take enjoyment from its contents. In any case, many thanks for simply giving it the time of day.

Jon Surtees
January 2013

SURREY CCC
On This Day

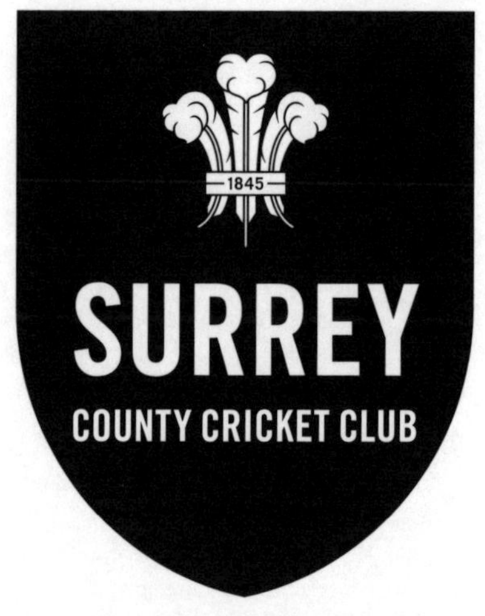

JANUARY

1st JANUARY 1910

Legendary Surrey pair Herbert Strudwick and 'Shrimp' Leveson-Gower were selected to make their England Test debuts against South Africa at Old Wanderers in Johannesburg. Strudwick claimed a stumping and a catch as England dismissed the hosts for 208. The day continued well for England as Surrey's Jack Hobbs opened the batting and ended 77*, just six shy of his then Test best of 83.

1st JANUARY 1959

Resuming on 89*, Peter May – at the time captain of England and Surrey and flushed with the success of the club's seventh consecutive County Championship – moved to 113 in a Test at the Melbourne Cricket Ground. The match also featured May's Surrey colleagues Tony Lock, Jim Laker and Peter Loader who – somewhat surprisingly – took only four wickets between them as Australia won by eight wickets.

1st JANUARY 1966

John Edrich got one of the greatest years in English sport off to a fine start with a century in the New Year Test at the Melbourne Cricket Ground. At the end of play in 1965, Surrey pair Edrich and Ken Barrington were well set on 48* and 54* respectively. Sadly for Barrington, he would only score another nine runs on New Year's Day but Edrich went on to an excellent 109. England secured a 200-run lead on the first innings but centuries on the last day from Peter Burge and Doug Walters saw the game end in a draw.

1st JANUARY 1997

The year got off to the worst possible start for Surrey when the hugely popular wicketkeeper Graham Kersey died of injuries suffered in a car crash on Boxing Day 1996. He was just 25. Kersey started his career at Kent but moved to Surrey in 1993 and played 49 times, taking 155 catches and averaging 22.52 with the bat as he frequently covered for Alec Stewart's England duty. His popularity at the club is borne out by the annual award for Team Man of the Year being renamed the Graham Kersey Award.

2nd JANUARY 1906

Surrey bowler Walter Lees came to his country's aid in Johannesburg. After winning the toss and choosing to bat, England were quickly reduced to 184 all out. However, opening the bowling, Lees put their efforts in the shade by taking four South African wickets to leave the hosts teetering on 71/8 overnight.

2nd JANUARY 1907

Laurie Fishlock was born near to The Oval in Battersea. Fishlock made his debut in 1931 and would go on to play for the club 347 times, making 22,138 runs at an excellent average of 40.47, including 50 centuries. He only played four Tests, caused by a combination of the Second World War wiping out six of what should have been his best years and some bad injury luck when selected on two Ashes tours in 1936/37 and 1946/47. In 1952, his final season for Surrey, 45-year-old Fishlock still made his 1,000 runs for the season and helped the club to the first of their record seven consecutive County Championship titles. Away from the cricket he was also a professional footballer and played on the wing for Crystal Palace and Southampton among others, as well as representing England as an amateur.

2nd JANUARY 1993

Tom Barling, a great Surrey batsman from 1927 to 1948, died aged 86 in Hastings. Barling played 389 games for the club, scoring 18,995 runs at 34.47, including 34 centuries. He shared a benefit year with Alf Gover in 1946, when he passed 2,000 runs in a season for the only time, including a memorable 233 against Nottinghamshire on a packed August Bank Holiday weekend.

2nd JANUARY 2003

England captain Nasser Hussain won the toss and chose to bat in the final Test at the Sydney Cricket Ground. Facing one of the greatest ever Australian sides, England were 4-0 down and staring a whitewash in the face. It didn't start well when Marcus Trescothick and Michael Vaughan both went cheaply but an innings of 124 from Surrey's Mark Butcher saved the day as England recovered to 264/5 overnight and went on to win by 225 runs.

3rd JANUARY 1912

'The Master' Jack Hobbs hit 126* as England powered to an eight-wicket victory in the second Ashes Test match at Melbourne. Australia added 30 to their overnight 269/8, leaving England needing 219 to win. Hobbs carried his bat in a comfortable victory.

3rd JANUARY 1920

Hobbs returned to the same ground eight years later, once again a second Test, and his performance was very similar. The Master was 53* overnight at the end of New Year's Day and – after a rest day – continued on to score 122. Sadly for his team the result was very different, with Australia winning the match by an innings and 91 runs on their way to a 5-0 series whitewash.

3rd JANUARY 1925

Five years later Hobbs was again back at the MCG. Australia had spent the first two days putting together 600 all out but Hobbs (154) and Herbert Sutcliffe (176) proved resolute in the face of a strong Aussie attack, batting all day to leave the score 283/0 overnight. England eventually conceded a lead of 121 on the first innings and, despite 127 in the second innings from Sutcliffe, lost a seven-day game by 81 runs.

4th JANUARY 1975

Geoff Arnold opened the bowling for England against Australia at the Sydney Cricket Ground. In a strong attack alongside his former Surrey colleague Bob Willis, Tony Greig, Derek Underwood and Fred Titmus – and under the leadership of John Edrich – Arnold took one of the four wickets to fall, Aussie captain Ian Chappell. The next day he would go on to take four more – including Chappell's brother Greg, his 100th Test scalp.

5th JANUARY 1971

John Edrich opened the batting alongside Geoffrey Boycott in the first ever one-day international, a 40-over game against Australia at the MCG. Edrich top scored in the match with 82 but saw his side fall to a five-wicket defeat with 42 balls remaining.

6th JANUARY 1960

England won the toss and batted in the first Test against the West Indies at the Kensington Oval, Bridgetown, Barbados. Surrey's Ken Barrington, at number three, anchored the day with 73*. He continued the following day to eventually make 128. Despite his effort, and a further hundred from Ted Dexter, 226 from Gary Sobers and 197* from Frank Worrell ensured the game finished in a draw.

7th JANUARY 1954

Alan Butcher, one of the club's longest-standing servants of the modern era, was born in Croydon. Butcher played 284 games for Surrey, scoring 14,605 runs at 33.34 with 29 centuries. He was unlucky to receive only one Test cap, against India at The Oval in 1979. As well as his long service as a batsman, Butcher was a Surrey coach for many years, and was head coach from 2006–2008. He is also the father of Surrey great Mark Butcher, as well as Gary Butcher, who played for the county too. In more recent years, Butcher has been the head coach of the Zimbabwe national side.

8th JANUARY 1882

Harry Primrose, Sixth Earl of Rosebery, was born. Captain of Surrey from 1905–1907, the man who was first addressed as Lord Dalmeny and then as Lord Lieutenant of Middleton was first a soldier – serving for all four years of the First World War – and then a politician. He served originally in the House of Commons, elected as a Liberal in 1906, and then entered the House of Lords in 1929. To wide surprise, his loyalty to Churchill's wartime coalition was honoured when he was appointed Secretary of State for Scotland and a member of the Privy Council in 1945. He also served as Surrey president from 1947–1949.

8th JANUARY 1966

After his 109 in the second Test, John Edrich picked up where he left off in the third, at the Sydney Cricket Ground. Coming into bat in the afternoon, he was 40* overnight and went on to score 103, helping set up a victory by an innings and 93 runs.

9th JANUARY 1975

Nine years on John Edrich – in his only game as England captain – returned to Sydney for another third Test. Despite an Edrich 50 in the first innings, England had conceded a large lead and were set 400 to win on the last day. At 33/0 overnight, they needed to bat out for a draw. They ended up losing by 171 runs but Edrich played a captain's knock, having his ribs broken by Dennis Lillee but returning to end 33* from 163 balls.

10th JANUARY 1991

Alec Stewart hit 55 as England lost a tight Benson & Hedges World Series one-day international to Australia at the MCG. Steve Waugh and Ian Healy took Australia to 222/6 and, despite Stewart's top score and a late effort from Angus Fraser, England fell tantalisingly short.

11th JANUARY 1895

Australian captain George Giffen won the toss and chose to bat in the third Test at Adelaide. However, his side were unable to capitalise as Surrey bowler Tom Richardson took 5-75 as they were dismissed for 238. However, that was as good the game got for England, who eventually lost by 382 runs.

11th JANUARY 1999

England played Sri Lanka at the Gabba in Brisbane. England captain Alec Stewart lost the toss and Sri Lanka batted first. However, The Gaffer was able to rely on his Surrey team-mate Adam Hollioake, who bowled brilliantly to take 3-32, setting up a four-wicket victory.

12th JANUARY 1959

Surrey spin duo Jim Laker and Tony Lock – under the leadership of their captain at both Surrey and England, Peter May – took the first three wickets as Australia replied to England's below-par 219. Laker (5-107) and Lock (4-130) would go on to take all bar one of the wickets to fall, before 92 from May in the second innings and 100 from Colin Cowdrey secured England a draw that saved them from a whitewash in the series.

13th JANUARY 1912

At the start of day two of the third Test in Adelaide, Jack Hobbs woke up 29* with England 49/0. The Master would bat for the vast majority of the day, putting on 147 for the first wicket with Wilfred Rhodes and then partnering with George Gunn, 'Young Jack' Hearne and Phil Mead before being dismissed late on by Roy Minnett for 187 with his side on 323.

13th JANUARY 2011

Surrey announced the signing of the man who was then the world's fastest bowler – Australian Shaun Tait – to play in that summer's Twenty20 competition. Sadly for both Surrey and cricket fans in England, Tait's injury problems would once again flare up with the bowling suffering an elbow injury while playing in the Indian Premier League for the Rajasthan Royals, forcing him to abandon the contract before even arriving in the country.

13th JANUARY 1930

On day one of the first Test at the Kensington Oval in Bridgetown, Barbados, the West Indies had proceeded to 338/8, a total which they increased to 369 on the morning of day two. England needed a strong first innings to avoid slipping behind and when Surrey's Andy Sandham batted for the remainder of the day to reach 111* they were in a good position. Sandham went on to make 152 as England secured a first-innings lead of 98 but 176 from the great George Headley in the West Indians' second innings left England 287 to win and, despite 51 from Sandham, the game ended in a draw with the tourists 167/3.

14th JANUARY 1962

Having conceded a big lead on the first innings, to stand any chance of victory in the crucial final Test match in Madras, England needed a big performance. The man to step up was Surrey's Tony Lock, who had already taken two wickets the previous evening. The leg-spinner took four more to complete figures of 6-65 and dismiss India for 190. This left England 338 to win, a target they missed by 128 runs.

14th JANUARY 1963

Martin Bicknell was born in Guildford. Bicknell would be considered one of the finest domestic fast bowlers of the modern era, taking 1,026 wickets for Surrey in 279 appearances. Further to this, one aspect of his game that was rarely given enough credit was his ability as a lower-order batsman, having scored 6,589 runs at 25.73 with three first-class centuries. He somehow only made four appearances in Test cricket – with England playing a record 114 matches in between his selections – but still took 14 wickets. A great club man, his older brother Darren also played 195 times for Surrey, averaging 40.20. After his retirement, Bicknell returned to Surrey, first as bowling coach and latterly as chief scout.

15th JANUARY 1908

With England chasing a massive target of 429 runs to beat Australia in a timeless match, there was very little chance of the feat being achieved. However Jack Hobbs, returning after being forced off the field with his score on just one, proved a match for the Aussie attack as he bravely came back out to bat with the score on 146/6, eventually ending injured but unbowed on 23*.

16th JANUARY 2011

Fresh from their glorious Ashes triumph, Surrey pair Chris Tremlett and Kevin Pietersen lined up against Australia in the first one-day international at the MCG, joined by a third Surrey player, Steven Davies, who had so far spent his winter carrying Matt Prior's gloves Down Under. Despite 78 from Pietersen and 42 from Davies, Australia came out victors by six wickets with five balls remaining.

17th JANUARY 1891

Walter Monckton, First Viscount Monckton of Brenchley, was born in Plaxtol, Kent. Monckton served two terms as Surrey president, from 1950–1952 and 1959–1964. Away from the club, he had a fascinating career, first serving as a legal adviser to Edward VIII during his abdication, then moving on to work in propaganda and information during the Second World War and becoming Solicitor General in the wartime cabinet. He continued to serve in the cabinet until 1957 and died seven years later in 1965.

18th JANUARY 1915

Captain Esme Fairfax Chinnery died in Issy, Paris. Chinnery played one match for Surrey, in 1906 against Oxford University at The Oval, scoring 47. During the First World War he served in the Royal Flying Corps and Coldsteam Guards but was killed while travelling over France as a passenger in a plane.

18th JANUARY 1992

England captain Graham Gooch won the toss and batted in the first Test against New Zealand in Christchurch. Gooch was dismissed early on but his opening partner, Alec Stewart, batted all day to score a brilliant 148 as England closed on 310/4. They went on to post 580 before bowling the hosts out twice to win by an innings and four runs.

19th JANUARY 1921

Needing 490 to beat Australia in the third Test at Adelaide, England were 66/1 overnight with Jack Hobbs 50*. Although they were unlikely to come near the required total, Hobbs still gave it his best shot with 123. Later in the day, Hobbs's Surrey colleague Percy Fender scored 42 from number eight – but both efforts were in vain as England lost by 119 runs.

19th JANUARY 1925

Hobbs returned to Adelaide four years later for an altogether tighter affair. Replying to the hosts' 489 in the first innings, Hobbs – down the order at number five – provided the solid base for England's innings, batting through day three to end 99* and going on to score 119.

19th JANUARY 1968

Colin Cowdrey won the toss and batted first in the opening Test of England's tour of the West Indies, held at Queen's Park Oval in Port-of-Spain. After the loss of Geoffrey Boycott and Surrey's John Edrich, the sturdy figure of Ken Barrington came in to bat at number four. By the end of the day he was 71* and had put on 134 with Cowdrey. He made 143, adding a further 188 with Tom Graveney.

20th JANUARY 1883

Surrey's Walter Read took a catch to dismiss George Bonnor off the bowling of Billy Bates during a Test at the Melbourne Cricket Ground. Although not normally something worth recording, Read's catch was actually one for the ages, coming after Bates's previous dismissals of Percy McDonnell and George Giffen to help his colleague record the first ever hat-trick in Test history.

20th JANUARY 1895

Born in Bushey, Hertfordshire, was Frank Chester, who has umpired no fewer than 12 Tests at The Oval, the most of any umpire. Following an exciting career as a teenage batsman at Worcestershire, Chester turned to umpiring after losing the bottom of his right arm in the First World War – using an artificial limb to make the correct signals. He was described by authorities no less than Sir Donald Bradman and E.W. Swanton as the greatest umpire of all time and his *Wisden* obituary said he 'raised umpiring to a higher level than had ever been known in the history of cricket'.

20th JANUARY 2011

Surrey announced the signing of young batsman Tom Maynard from Glamorgan. Maynard had decided to leave the Welsh club after internal politics caused his father, former England batsman Matthew, to leave his post as head coach of the club. Considered at the time to be one of the finest young players in the English game, Maynard was brilliant in the season and a half he played for Surrey before his tragic death the following year.

21st JANUARY 1865

Bill Brockwell was born in Kingston-upon-Thames. Brockwell, whose Surrey chances were initially limited by the brilliance of Tom Richardson and George Lohmann, made his debut for Surrey in 1886. Starting out as a fast-medium bowler, he took exactly 500 wickets at an average of 24.54 from his 314 matches. However, later in his career he shone more with the bat, combining with Bobby Abel and Tom Hayward on some superb Oval pitches. He retired in 1900, having scored 11,830 runs at an average of 27.70. Brockwell also played seven Tests, all against Australia.

22nd JANUARY 1948

In the first Test at the Kensington Oval, the West Indies had prevailed on the first day, ending on 244/3. Surrey's Jim Laker, on his Test debut, had taken one wicket with Maurice Tremlett – who eight years later would sire son Tim, who would in turn father Chris in 1981 – also taking a wicket. However, the game was changed early on the second morning, with Laker finding formidable turn and making a sizeable early impact on the international scene as he took six of the last seven wickets to fall to complete figures of 7/103.

23rd JANUARY 1962

Early in his career, a very young Ken Barrington was assessed by the then Surrey coach Andy Sandham as a leg-spinner. The coach decided his deliveries lacked accuracy and – with Lock and Laker bowling in tandem – there was no real requirement for another spinner and therefore told him to concentrate on his batting. Fast forward 15 years and England were playing Pakistan in the second Test at Dacca. The pitch was a spinner's paradise – Surrey's Tony Lock took 4/70 from his 42 overs – but more noteworthy was Barrington's stint of 21 overs for just 17 runs with 13 maidens. A great man – and a man of many talents.

24th JANUARY 1950

Stan Squires, one of only 15 men to play more than 400 first-class games for Surrey, died at the Old Deer Park in Richmond, aged 40. Primarily a right-handed batsman, Squires hit 18,636 runs for Surrey at an average of 31.11 but he was also a fine bowler of off-breaks, taking 297 wickets at 35.34. He played for the club from 1928 to 1949, serving with the Royal Air Force during the Second World War before returning to the side in 1946. His final game for Surrey, against 'The Rest' in Kingston-upon-Thames, was just over four months before his tragic early death, from a blood virus. However – a renowned multi-sportsman who was also a boxer, footballer, squash and rugby player – Squires won a golf foursome competition for his club just months before he passed away.

25th JANUARY 1973

Surrey's Graham Roope made his Test debut when selected for England's fourth Test against India in Kanpur. It was an uneventful first day for Roope, as India batted and proceeded to 168/2 at the close of play. The match was eventually drawn, with Roope opening the batting with Mike Denness and scoring 11. He played 21 Tests for England, scoring 860 runs at an average of 30.71.

25th JANUARY 1997

Replying to New Zealand's 390 all out in the first Test at Auckland, Alec Stewart ended this particular day on 67*. He went on to make 173 – with Graham Thorpe adding a further 119 across the next two days. At the start of the final day New Zealand needed another 75 runs just to make England bat again but Michael Atherton's side were eventually denied a seemingly inevitable victory by a near three-hour partnership between New Zealand's last-wicket pair Nathan Astle and Danny Morrison, who batted for 166 minutes.

THE LATE SURREY BATSMAN TOM MAYNARD

26th JANUARY 1983

Surrey batsman John 'Jack' Parker died in Bromley, aged 69. Parker played 334 times for Surrey, scoring 14,068 runs at an average of 31.82. He made his debut for the club against Glamorgan in 1932 – alongside Jack Hobbs and Andy Sandham – and played until the end of the 1952 season, retiring on a high as Surrey won the County Championship with a side including the Bedser twins, Peter May, Stuart Surridge, Jim Laker and Tony Lock. He never played Test cricket, but was selected for the England squad to tour India in 1939/40, a trip that never happened because of the eventual outbreak of the Second World War.

26th JANUARY 2004

Surrey announced the biggest sponsorship contract in the history of domestic cricket when Brit Insurance agreed a £500,000-a-year deal which changed the name of the ground to the Brit Oval and saw the company's logo displayed on Surrey shirts. The previous deal, with AMP, had been worth around £350,000 a year.

27th JANUARY 2009

The club announced the signing of fast bowler Chris Tremlett from Hampshire. Tremlett, aged 28 at the time, had taken 289 wickets at 28.66 and represented England in all three forms of the game. Surrey team director Chris Adams commented that he thought Tremlett 'had all the right attributes to continue his England career', an opinion that proved to be true when the 6ft 7in seamer bowled his country to victory in an Ashes series on Australian soil two years later.

28th JANUARY 1880

Herbert 'Bert' Strudwick was born in Mitcham. One of the finest wicketkeepers of all time, Strudwick played 554 matches for the club (and sits third on the all-time list), took 1,035 catches for Surrey (322 more than Edward Brooks in second place), and claimed 187 stumpings (incongruously, only second on the all-time list behind Ted Pooley). However, in the modern game – where a wicketkeeper is expected to also bat very well – Strudwick may have struggled as he regularly batted at number 11 and only managed to score 5,485 runs at 11.01 for Surrey, also registering a record 107 ducks for the club (20 more than Pat Pocock in second place). In the Test arena he played 28 times for England, taking 61 catches, making 12 stumpings and scoring 230 runs at an average of just 7.93. After his retirement in 1927 he remained involved with the club, coaching and becoming scorer – he also famously contributed a number of articles to the *Wisden Almanack* up until his death – in Shoreham-by-Sea, Sussex, in 1970.

28th JANUARY 2002

England were soundly beaten by India in the fourth one-day international of the series in Kanpur. England scored 218/7 from their 39 overs, a total India comfortably surpassed from just 29.4, with Sachin Tendulkar scoring 87 from 67 balls. The Surrey contribution was 36* from Graham Thorpe and 13 and 0-33 from Ben Hollioake. It would normally be recorded as an otherwise unremarkable match but it was to be all-rounder Hollioake's last official game of cricket as he would be tragically killed in a car accident less than two months later.

29th JANUARY 1892

Surrey's George Lohmann took 8-58 in the first Test in Sydney to dismiss Australia for 144. By the end of the day, Bobby Abel was 23* after opening with W.G. Grace. He would go on to record his Test best of 132*.

29th JANUARY 1998

The first day of the first Test between England and the West Indies at Sabina Park, Kingston. Michael Atherton won the toss and chose to bat, walking out alongside Alec Stewart. After 45 minutes, England were 17/3 and Stewart was black and blue following ten overs from Courtney Walsh and Curtly Ambrose on a pitch described by match referee Barry Jarman as 'horrific'. The second Surrey batsman to make it to the crease, Mark Butcher, was mercifully dismissed first ball but Stewart – who faced 26 balls – and Graham Thorpe – who faced ten – were less lucky. Eventually the game became the first in Test history to be called off because of the state of the pitch.

30th JANUARY 1963

Australia started the final day of the fourth Test in Adelaide 287 runs ahead with four wickets in hand. Brian Statham and Fred Trueman kept them to just 293 but England still had a large part of the day to bat out. When openers Geoff Pullar and David Sheppard were dismissed to leave England 4/2, the worst was feared. However, Ken Barrington played a magnificent innings from number three, batting for the rest of the day to score 132* and secure the draw.

31st JANUARY 1887

After being dismissed for just 45 in the first innings England were on shaky ground at Sydney. When they conceded a first-innings lead of 74 it looked worse. However, a total of 184 in the second innings – to which Surrey's Maurice Read only contributed a first-ball duck – left the hosts needing 111. They were dismissed for 97. The main weapon of attack was

Nottinghamshire's Billy Barnes but Surrey bowler George Lohmann acted as a perfect foil, taking 3/20 as England secured a brilliant 13-run victory.

GEORGE LOHMANN, WHO REPRESENTED THE CLUB FROM 1884 TO 1896

SURREY CCC
On This Day

FEBRUARY

1st FEBRUARY 1873

Sir Henry Dudley Gresham Leveson-Gower died in Kensington. Throughout his playing days he was known universally by his schoolboy nickname 'Shrimp' but is now widely referred to as simply H.D.G. He made his Surrey debut in 1895 and continued to play for the club until 1920, clocking up 122 appearances and 3,308 runs at 22.50. He also played three Tests, averaging 23.75, and actually became an England selector in 1909, during his playing career. After his final match for Surrey he became club treasurer from 1926–1928 and president from 1929–1939 as well as serving as chairman of England's selectors in 1924 and then 1927–1930. He was knighted for services to cricket in 1953, the same year as Sir Jack Hobbs. Away from the cricket field, he also served as a major in the Royal Army Service Corps during the First World War, and was mentioned in dispatches.

2nd FEBRUARY 1951

When Alec Bedser opened the bowling in the fourth Test in Adelaide and removed Ken Archer without a run scored, the side – 3-0 down in the series – might have thought their luck had changed. Sadly not, although Bedser contributed one more wicket that day, as Australia ended on 254/3 and won by 274 runs.

3rd FEBRUARY 1974

After being skittled for 131 in the first innings, England needed a big performance from their bowlers to get them back into the first Test against the West Indies at Port-of-Spain. This did not happen but it could have been a lot worse were it not for Surrey's Pat Pocock who bowled Rohan Kanhai and had Deryck Murray caught by Keith Fletcher. He would continue the next day and finish with 5-110.

4th FEBRUARY 1995

England ended the second day of the final Test in Perth on 110/4, chasing Australia's total of 402. Graham Thorpe was 54* and Mark Ramprakash (then of Middlesex) 14*. In a very chastening series for England, the pair continued to show defiance with Thorpe eventually making 123, just the second England century that series.

5th FEBRUARY 1872

The Oval hosted the first international rugby match, between England and Scotland. The attendance was recorded as 4,000 and the game bore little relation to what might be seen today, with 20 players on each side and the final score reading England 2G Scotland 1G. England scored three tries, via Francis d'Aguilar, Stephen Finney and Alfred Hammersley, and a drop goal from Harold Freeman. Scotland scored no tries, their only score a drop goal from Charles Cathcart. Contrary to popular belief, the match was not played for the Calcutta Cup – with six more games before it was introduced in 1879.

6th FEBRUARY 1992

England won the toss and batted in the third Test against New Zealand in Wellington. Looking to tie up a 3-0 whitewash, Alec Stewart, opening alongside captain Graham Gooch, was the mainstay of the first innings, scoring 107 as England posted 239/5 at the end of the day.

7th FEBRUARY 1997

England returned to Wellington – this time for the second Test. After bowling their hosts out for 124 in the first innings, they spent the second day proceeding to 204/3, with Graham Thorpe 47* overnight. He would go on the next day to score 108 and England won by an innings and 68 runs.

8th FEBRUARY 1968

Colin Cowdrey won the toss and chose to bat in the second Test at Port-of-Spain. By the end of the first day, England had reached 222/2, the lion's share of which had been scored by John Edrich, who was caught by Rohan Kanhai off the bowling of Gary Sobers for 96.

9th FEBRUARY 1922

Jim Laker was born in Frizinghall, Yorkshire. As a young man he attended nets at Headingley and was recommended as a batsman. The outbreak of the Second World War put a temporary stop to his career. After returning from the war, he settled on the outskirts of London and – after Yorkshire gave permission – was recommended to Surrey and never looked back.

9th FEBRUARY 2010

Surrey announced that, following four years being known as the Surrey Brown Caps in limited overs cricket, they would return to their previous moniker, the Surrey Lions. Surrey team director Chris Adams said he hoped the name change would 'bring a bit of bite back to the team'.

10th FEBRUARY 1912

England started the second day of the fourth Test at the MCG at 54/0 after bowling Australia out for 191. Jack Hobbs was 30* and would spend almost the entire second day batting alongside Wilfred Rhodes (179) as the pair put on 323 for the first wicket before Hobbs was dismissed for 178. The partnership remains the second-highest opening partnership ever for England and the 11th of all time.

10th FEBRUARY 1960

Surrey wicketkeeper Edward 'Ted' Brooks died in Rustington, Sussex, aged 61. Brooks originally joined the Surrey staff as a medium-pace bowler but kept wicket in a minor match in 1923 and did so well he concentrated on that from then on in. He made his first-class debut in 1925 and went on to to claim 810 dismissals, second only to Bert Strudwick. A sometimes useful lower-order batsman, he still holds the club record for the highest ever ninth-wicket partnership – of 168 with Errol Holmes – against Hampshire in 1936.

10th FEBRUARY 1961

Popular and powerful batsman David Ward was born in Croydon. Ward played 155 times for Surrey, scoring 8,078 runs and averaging 38.46. The purveyor of a heavy bat and fantastic eye for the ball, Ward was originally a carpenter and did not make his Surrey debut until the age of 24. His best year was 1990 when he scored 2,072 runs in 34 first-class innings at an average of 76.74, including seven centuries. Ward was also an excellent limited overs batsman, scoring 5,178 runs at 30.63 including 15 centuries. His aggregate of 968 List A runs in 1994 is the second-highest in club history. After his retirement in 2001, he is now a cricket coach at Whitgift School in Croydon.

11th FEBRUARY 1970

Alistair Brown, the leading one-day run-scorer in Surrey's history, was born in Beckenham, Kent. After attending Caterham School, the man known throughout the game as simply 'The Lord' made his Surrey debut in 1990 and his first-class debut two years later. An immensely popular figure with fans throughout his 18 years of first-team cricket, he remains the only man to ever hit two double centuries in one-day cricket and holds the world one-day record of 268, an achievement honoured at The Oval by the Ali Brown 268 Bar in the Long Room. He also still holds the record for the highest one-day opening partnership in Surrey history, 294 with James Benning in the famous match with Gloucestershire in 2007. In first-class cricket, he scored 14,864 runs for Surrey at an average of 43.20; in one-day cricket he added a further 10,358 at 32.16, the only man to ever hit more than 10,000 career one-day runs. Most observers accept that his 16 one-day internationals were far too few for his ability and he is considered one of the finest English cricketers to never play a Test. After leaving the club in 2008 he ended his career with three seasons at Nottinghamshire before returning to Surrey to become second XI coach, a position he currently holds.

12th FEBRUARY 1921

After England made 284 against Australia in the fourth Test at Melbourne (with 27 from Jack Hobbs), Australia were looking to secure a good first-innings lead. By the end of day two they trailed by just three runs with five wickets in hand. This was despite the sterling efforts of Percy Fender, who took three wickets – including Johnny Taylor, who went hit wicket. The following day, he would go on to take two more, finishing with 5-122.

13th FEBRUARY 1993

Chasing a giant 560 in the second Test against India in Madras, England started the day on 19/0 with Robin Smith and captain Alec Stewart at the crease. While not a brilliant day for the tourists – who end on 221/7 – Stewart distinguished himself with a 269-ball vigil for 74, putting on over 100 with Graeme Hick before England collapsed after his dismissal.

14th FEBRUARY 1896

George Lohmann takes the fourth hat-trick in international cricket during the first Test between England and South Africa at St George's Park, Port Elizabeth. Lohmann's treble was the final act of a two-day England win, as he took the final three wickets to fall, the last – Joseph Willoughby – caught by his debuting Surrey colleague Tom Hayward.

14th FEBRUARY 1909

Surrey secretary and president Geoffrey Howard was born in Hampstead Garden Suburb. His professional career was a short one, consisting of three matches for Middlesex. However, it was as a cricket administrator, first with Surrey as assistant secretary, Lancashire and back to Surrey, that he excelled. He ran the club from 1965 to 1974 and was also tour manager for England abroad, memorably during the 1954/55 Ashes victory. He stayed involved with the club and served as president in 1989 before dying aged 93 in November 2002.

15th FEBRUARY 1965

With the series tied at 1-1, crowds were anticipating an exciting final Test at the Sydney Cricket Ground. It was not to be with England and Australia playing out a dull draw that was roundly criticised from all sides. However, the first day saw another fine performance from Ken Barrington who, according to a report from the time, was 'entrenched' at one end on the first day as he compiled his 101.

16th FEBRUARY 1886

Andy Ducat, one of Surrey's greatest batsmen of the early 20th century, was born in Brixton. As well as playing 422 times for Surrey, Ducat is one of only 12 men to have represented their country at cricket and football. For Surrey, Ducat scored 23,108 runs at 38.64 – including 306* against Oxford University in 1919 and 51 other centuries. His only Test match was against Australia at Headingley in 1921 where he was unlucky to only score three and two. On the football pitch he joined Woolwich Arsenal in 1905 before switching to Aston Villa in 1912 and then Fulham in 1921. He made 313 club appearances and a further six for England.

17th FEBRUARY 1998

In the third Test at Port-of-Spain, England had been set 225 to beat the West Indies. Although the score seems low on paper, it would have been comfortably the highest in the match. No visiting side had won at Port -of-Spain for 21 years but, with Alec Stewart scoring 83, England started the final day 41 runs from victory. Mark Butcher was 24* and played the key role, shepherding England home in the face of Curtly Ambrose and Courtney Walsh bowling at their absolute peak as they secured a famous three-wicket win.

18th FEBRUARY 1829

The birth of Surrey president William John Monson, First Viscount Oxenbridge, also known as The Lord Monson. He was the club's fourth president and served from 1879–1894. Monson had no cricket career but was very well connected, serving under Gladstone as Treasurer of the Household and then Captain Yeoman of the Guard before he joined the Privy Council in 1874. He died on 16th April 1898.

19th FEBRUARY 1921

Bernard 'Bernie' Constable was born in East Molesey, Surrey. Constable played 434 times for Surrey, scoring 18,224 runs at 30.37 and also contributing 49 wickets. He made his first-class debut in 1939, playing two matches before seeing the next six seasons wiped out by the Second World War. Before he retired in 1964 he was a key member of the side that won seven consecutive County Championships and gained a fine honour when Micky Stewart said that he had 'learned more about cricket from Bernie Constable than from anyone else'. He died, aged 76, in 1997.

20th FEBRUARY 2008

The Oval was officially recommended as a venue for the 2009 World Twenty20. The ground would host nine matches in the tournament, including the semi-final where the eventual runners-up, Sri Lanka, beat the West Indies by 57 runs. The highlight of the many fireworks seen at the ground the following June was the 88 scored by Chris Gayle against Australia, which featured six of the largest sixes ever seen at The Oval.

21st FEBRUARY 1908

Surrey's Jack Crawford (3-52) provided valuable support to Sydney Barnes as England dismissed Australia for just 137 in the fifth Test at the Sydney Cricket Ground. Jack Hobbs then opened the innings, racing to 65* overnight as England ended the day on 116/1.

22nd FEBRUARY 1909

Surrey great Stan Squires was born in Kingston-upon-Thames. Squires played 402 games, abandoning an early career in the City after his lessons with South African Test star Aubrey Faulkner paid off and he was picked up by Surrey. His *Wisden* obituary said that 'no more popular player wore the Surrey colours' than Squires.

23rd FEBRUARY 1951

Alec Bedser took four wickets as England started the fifth Ashes Test at the Melbourne Cricket Ground by reducing Australia to 206/8 overnight. Bedser would complete his five-for the following morning, adding another five in the second innings as England won by eight wickets to avoid a whitewash. Amazingly, these are the only occasions on which Bedser took five wickets in a Test innings outside England.

24th FEBRUARY 1990

Alec Stewart, ultimately England's most capped Test cricketer, made his Test debut at Sabina Park, Kingston – alongside another future England captain, Nasser Hussain. With Jack Russell in the side, Stewart was not required to keep wicket and made a quiet debut, scoring 13 in England's brilliant nine-wicket victory that he was at the crease, alongside Wayne Larkins, to experience.

25th FEBRUARY 2001

Sir Donald Bradman died at his home in Adelaide at the age of 92. 'The Don', as he was known to all cricket fans around the world, is one of the greatest figures in the history of Australia. In England, his career will be forever associated with The Oval, where he played four innings, scoring 232, 244, 77 and, famously, a duck in his last ever Test innings. His total of 553 Test runs at The Oval remains a record for a non-Englishman today.

26th FEBRUARY 1921

Australia began day two of the fifth Ashes Test at the Sydney Cricket Ground on 70/2, looking to overhaul England's 204. By the end of the day they had scored 392 all out and left England 24/2. However, the leading Englishman on the day was Percy Fender, who stuck to his task to record excellent figures of 5/90.

27th FEBRUARY 2011

Surrey wicketkeeper Steven Davies announced that he is gay, becoming the first current international in a team sport to do so. He was immediately supported by his Surrey and England team-mates and received acclamation from the sporting world for his brave decision. Speaking to the *Daily Telegraph*, Davies said: 'I'm comfortable with who I am – and happy to say who I am in public. This is the right time for me…I feel it is right to be out in the open about my sexuality. If more people do it, the more acceptable it will become. That must be a good thing. To speak out is a massive relief for me, but if I can just help one person to deal with their sexuality then that's all I care about. It was a fantastic thing to do, telling the lads. The difference is huge. I am so much happier.' The announcement was of no concern to England coach Andy Flower who added: 'Steve's private life is his own concern. It has absolutely no bearing on his ability to excel at the very highest level in international sport.'

28th FEBRUARY 1959

In the first Test against New Zealand at Christchurch, Tony Lock took 5-31 as England whipped their hosts out for just 142. Lock would take 6-53 in the second innings with England taking a crushing victory by an innings and 99 runs.

29th FEBRUARY 1968

The Leap Year day saw Surrey off-spinner Pat Pocock make his Test debut for England against the West Indies at the Kensington Oval, Barbados. It was a quiet first day for Pocock, as rain meant the hosts moved to just 86/2 at the end of day one.

ALEC STEWART BATTING AT THE START OF HIS INTERNATIONAL CAREER

SURREY CCC
On This Day

MARCH

1st MARCH 1898

At the end of day two of the fifth Ashes Test at the Sydney Cricket Ground, Australia were 184/5, trailing England by 151 runs. Surrey's Tom Richardson had already taken four of the first five wickets to fall and repeated the feat when he took four of the last five as well, finishing with his Test best figures of 8/94. The day continued well for Surrey players with Tom Hayward top scoring with 43 in the English second innings.

2nd MARCH 1896

England captain Lord Hawke won the toss and batted in the second Test against South Africa at Johannesburg. Sir Tim O'Brien (0) and Surrey's George Lohmann (2) – who curiously opened the innings despite a Test average of just 8.8 with the bat – were dismissed cheaply but 122 from Tom Hayward, described as a 'fine display' by the ever-present *Wisden* reporter, helped England to 355/7 at the close.

2nd MARCH 1968

Once England had dismissed the West Indies for 349 in their first innings at the Kensington Oval (with a wicket each for Ken Barrington and Pat Pocock), opening pair John Edrich and Geoff Boycott took over. On this occasion it was Edrich that shone the brightest, reaching the end of the day 64* and going on to score 146.

3rd MARCH 1986

Jade Winston Dernbach was born in Johannesburg. Although South African by birth, Dernbach learnt his cricket at Guildford CC before being guided through the Surrey youth system and making his first-class debut in 2003 against India A. He made his England debut in a Twenty20 international in 2011 against Sri Lanka at the County Ground, Bristol, before making his one-day international debut three days later at The Oval.

4th MARCH 2009

Ian Salisbury rejoined Surrey as second XI coach after initially leaving in 2007. After winning the Second XI Championship in his first season in charge, Salisbury was promoted and is now first-team coach.

5th MARCH 1870

England played 'Scotland' in the first ever international football match, held at The Oval. The match was initiated by Surrey secretary C.W. Alcock, who wrote the following letter to the *Glasgow Herald* attempting to recruit Scottish players: 'FOOTBALL. ENGLAND V SCOTLAND. Sir, will you allow me a few lines in your newspaper to notify to Scotch players that a match under the above title will take place in London on Sat 10th inst., according to the rules of the Football Association. It is the object of the committee to select the best elevens at their disposal in the two countries, and I cannot but think that the appearance of some of the more prominent celebrities of football on the northern side of the Tweed would do much to disseminate a healthy feeling of good fellowship among the contestants and tend to promote a still greater extent the extension of the game...' Alcock skippered the England side with Scotland being led by James Kirkpatrick. Scotland took a late lead through Robert Crawford but Alfred Baker equalised for England with one minute remaining to secure a 1-1 draw. The match has not been recognised as a full international by FIFA, along with four subsequent fixtures all at The Oval, because the Scottish players were all London-based Scots and therefore not a full national side.

6th MARCH 1998

An unheralded youngster by the name of Kevin Peter Pietersen made his first-class debut for Natal B against Easterns in the UCB Bowl. It was a quiet day for the man who would become 'KP' and join Surrey in 2010, taking the wicket of Craig Norris and not batting, largely because he was selected more as a bowler and was not due to come in until number eight.

7th MARCH 2011

Richard Gould was appointed chief executive of Surrey CCC. Gould, formerly a major in the Royal Tank Regiment, commercial director of Bristol City FC and chief executive of Somerset CCC, replaced Paul Sheldon who had been in charge at the club since 1995. In a boost for journalists looking for a good angle on an otherwise relatively dull story, he was also the son of former Wales and Wimbledon manager Bobby Gould.

8th MARCH 1873

The first ever officially recognised international football match in England was staged at The Oval. England won 4-2, with the first goal scored by William Kenyon-Slaney – now officially recognised as England's first ever goal.

8th MARCH 1929

England captain Jack White won the toss and batted in the final Ashes Test at the Melbourne Cricket Ground. In his final Test in Australia, Jack Hobbs was characteristically brilliant, batting almost all day to score 142 and giving a young Australian named Donald Bradman a long day in the field. Bradman would serve notice of his potential though, scoring 123 in the first innings as Australia won a consolation victory by five wickets.

9th MARCH 1992

Alec Stewart, kept wicket for England in a World Cup match against Sri Lanka at the Eastern Oval in Ballarat. He contributed 59 from 37 balls to England's 280/6 and then caught Arjuna Ranatunga off the bowling of Ian Botham as Graham Gooch's side recorded a 106-run victory.

10th MARCH 1845

William Houghton, of Brixton Hill, president of the Montpelier Club, became the new lessee of a Kennington market garden belonging to the Duchy of Cornwall that for the previous ten years was being lined up for a new housing development. His plan was to turn it into a 'Subscription Cricket Ground'. The club required a new ground because their previous facility, the grounds of the Bee Hive Tavern at Walworth, was required for building. The negotiations were conducted by the treasurer of the Montpelier Club, Mr W. Baker, and William Ward MP, who had already successfully prevented Lord's from being built on. The first match took place in May that year after 10,000 turves from Tooting Common had been laid due to the fact that, at that stage, The Oval was 'in a most ruinous condition and from the effluvium arising from decayed vegetables a nuisance and a source of ill-health'. The ground was still studded with trees though, as permission to cut some of them down was not granted until 1847.

11th MARCH 1910

Frederick Fane won the toss and chose to bat in the glorious shadow of Table Mountain at Newlands in Cape Town. The decision paid off handsomely as Jack Hobbs made hay, scoring 187 before being given out hit wicket to Pompey Norton. Once again, Hobbs put on runs with Wilfred Rhodes, with *Wisden* reporting the great Yorkshireman was 'overshadowed by his partner's brilliancy' as he scored 'just' 77. By the end of the day, England were 406/7 and would go on to win the match by nine wickets.

12th MARCH 1906

Walter Lees took the final three South African wickets to fall in their first innings at Old Wanderers, Johannesburg to record his Test best figures of 6-78. Later in the day, Ernie Hayes scored 35 in the English first innings. The second innings saw Lees add three more wickets and Hayes remained unbeaten on 11* despite England slipping to defeat by 243 runs to complete a 4-1 series reverse.

12th MARCH 1998

England opened the fifth Test against the West Indies at the Kensington Oval in Barbados by being asked to bat first by rival captain Brian Lara. Courtney Walsh removed Alec Stewart (12) and Michael Atherton (11) early and when Nasser Hussain (5) and Mark Butcher (19) also went, England were in deep trouble. However, Mark Ramprakash – whose incredible Surrey career was not yet a glint in the eye of even the most ardent fan – and Graham Thorpe batted brilliantly. Surrey man Thorpe was struck down by a back spasm but returned when Jack Russell was out and at the end of the day, Ramprakash was 80* and Thorpe 50*. Thorpe would go on to make a typically determined 103, with the mercurial Ramprakash recording a Test best of 154.

13th MARCH 1981

At the Kensington Oval, Barbados, Robin Jackman – a Surrey hero beloved by members for his passion and loud, insistent appealing – was handed his Test debut. Jackman did very well, dismissing Gordon Greenidge, Desmond Haynes and Clive Lloyd on his way to first-day figures of 3-65.

14th MARCH 1981

Surrey and England legend Ken Barrington was found dead in his room on England's tour of the West Indies after suffering a heart attack. Robin Jackman, due to play the second day of his Test debut, admitted he could not bowl properly because he had tears in his eyes. Barrington's body was flown back to England by his wife Ann and he was cremated in Leatherhead on 21st March. Over 150 wreaths were received, including one from all 16 other county clubs.

15th MARCH 1960

Raman Subba Row hit exactly 100 for England against the West Indies in the drawn fourth Test at Georgetown. Subba Row played 41 games for Surrey before leaving at the end of 1954 to go to Northamptonshire. He would return to The Oval in retirement, serving as Surrey chairman from 1974 to 1978 and chairing the club's management board from 1979–1992. He was chairman of the Test and County Cricket Board (now known as the England and Wales Cricket Board) from 1986–1990 and became a Test referee.

15th MARCH 2002

Graham Thorpe hit his Test best of 200* in a day against New Zealand at Jade Stadium in Christchurch. Coming in with the score 85/4, Thorpe was partnered by Andrew Flintoff, who hit 137. The two scored quickly, with Thorpe's superb innings coming from just 231 balls. England eventually declared on 468/6, setting New Zealand 550 to win. They came close though, scoring 451 all out to lose by 98 runs, with Nathan Astle hitting a memorable 222 from 168 balls before he was last out.

15th MARCH 2011

Great fast bowler Peter Loader died in Perth, aged 81. Loader, born in Wallington, emigrated to Australia after his retirement in 1963. He took 1,108 wickets for the club at an average of 19.04. He also took 39 Test wickets at 22.51 including England's first post-war hat-trick against the West Indies at Headingley in 1957. Surrey chairman Richard Thompson declared Loader's passing 'a real loss to the club'.

16th MARCH 1872

The first ever FA Cup Final was staged at The Oval, pitching Wanderers against the Royal Engineers. Wanderers became the first name on the trophy, Morton Betts scoring the only goal in a 1-0 triumph watched by 2,000.

16th MARCH 1971

Australian left-arm spinner Chuck Fleetwood-Smith died in Fitzroy, Melbourne, aged 62. Fleetwood-Smith played one Test at The Oval and has the odd distinction of being the bowler to concede the most runs in a single innings of Test cricket. During the final Ashes Test of 1938, Fleetwood-Smith sent down 87 overs, conceding 298 runs and taking just one wicket, England captain Wally Hammond. The prime destructive influence was Len Hutton, who hit 364* as England accumulated 903/7 over two and a half days.

17th MARCH 2001

One of the most extraordinary days in the history of Graham Thorpe's long Test career. England started what would become the final day of the third Test in Colombo on 175/4, with Thorpe 71*. Although he made a brilliant 113*, his side's eventual total of 249 gave them just an eight-run lead. However, when Sri Lanka were dismissed for just 81 from 28.1 overs England suddenly needed only 74 to win the match and complete a previously unthought-of series win in Sri Lanka. When Alec Stewart fell at 43/4 though, Thorpe – still dizzy with fatigue from his first-innings effort when he walked to the crease – was the last senior batsman remaining. He would rarely make a more vital 32*, seeing his side home to a memorable victory that caused Darren Gough to shout the immortal line: 'It's time to go and get absolutely hammered!'

GRAHAM THORPE, WHO SCORED 12,054 RUNS FOR SURREY

18th MARCH 1997

Alec Bedser was invited to Buckingham Palace to collect his knighthood from Her Majesty Queen Elizabeth II. He was the 16th man knighted for his services to cricket and first ever specialist bowler, putting the lie to a phrase he was known to be fond of repeating: 'The last bowler to be knighted was Sir Francis Drake.'

19th MARCH 1892

Twenty years on from the first game, West Bromwich Albion and Aston Villa played out a Birmingham derby in the last FA Cup Final to be staged at The Oval. The game ended 3-0 to West Brom with goals from Jasper Geddes, Sammy Nicholls and Jack Reynolds. It was the first final where goal nets were used.

19th MARCH 1973

England and Warwickshire left-arm spinner Ashley Giles was born in Chertsey. Although Giles was lionised for his feats in the West Midlands, his cricketing homeland is Surrey and he learned the game at Ripley and Guildford CC, playing his first match for the Surrey second XI in 1990 in a side that also contained Mark Butcher and Adam Hollioake. He played a further match in 1991 – with Alistair Brown now added to the side – before making his first-class debut for Warwickshire in 1993 and his Test match debut in 1998. Giles, known to millions of England cricket fans as 'The King of Spain' following an unfortunate printing error in 2004, is now the England one-day coach.

20th MARCH 1973

A hard day in the field for England as they played Pakistan in the second Test at Hyderabad. Majid Khan's Pakistan started on 266/4 and proceeded to 561/9 at stumps. In the meantime Pat Pocock took two of the four wickets he would claim in the innings and Geoff Arnold cleaned bowled his Surrey colleague Intikhab Alam, but not until the great man had completed his only Test century of 138.

21st MARCH 2011

Surrey announced that South African fast bowler Andre Nel would not fulfil the final year of his contract. Nel played two seasons for the club, taking 48 wickets at 29.68 but was hampered by a series of injuries. He was also, inevitably, known for his on-field persona of 'Gunther' – allegedly a mountain man from Germany – that brought a huge passion to his performances and, on more than one occasion, caused loud swear words to echo off the Oval gasholder and around the cavernous OCS Stand.

22nd MARCH 2009

Surrey played Middlesex in an unusual London derby, at Sharjah in the United Arab Emirates. Although offering good pre-season experience, the result did not go south of the river as Scott Newman's 56 was bettered by Billy Godleman's 68 and Middlesex won by two wickets.

23rd MARCH 1906

Fast bowler Maurice Allom was born in Northwood, Middlesex. Allom played 100 times for Surrey, taking 333 wickets at 22.66. He made his debut in 1927 and his England Test debut three years later at Lancaster Park in Christchurch against New Zealand, becoming one of only three players to take a hat-trick on his debut and the first ever to take four wickets in five balls. After retiring in 1938, he served as Surrey president from 1970–1977 and his son Anthony played one first-class game for the club in 1960.

23rd MARCH 2002

Tragedy came for the second time in five years when young all-rounder Ben Hollioake was killed in a car crash in Perth, Australia. Hollioake, the younger brother of club captain Adam, was an extraordinary talent. His first-class averages of 25.87 with the bat and 33.45 with the ball do no justice to his potential, which was underscored by the amazing 63 he scored from 48 balls on his international debut against Australia at Lord's in 1997. A frequent headline-grabber, Hollioake was also the master of the big occasion, named Man of the Match each time he made it to the Benson and Hedges Cup Final in 1997 and 2001. Speaking at his funeral in Fremantle, his brother Adam described Ben as 'too cool to get old' and, later in the year, Surrey and England team-mate Mark Butcher performed 'You're Never Gone', a song he wrote in tribute to Ben.

24th MARCH 2009

Surrey lost to Sussex by six wickets in the PROArch Trophy. Captain Michael Brown, a new arrival from Hampshire, scored 101 as Surrey totalled 255 but 110 from Sussex's Joe Gatting saw the south coast rivals ease to victory.

25th MARCH 1868

Fast bowler William Henry 'Bill' Lockwood was born in Old Radford, Nottinghamshire. Lockwood is best known for bowling in tandem with Tom Richardson in the great Surrey sides of the late 19th century. He was characterised by a very heavy delivery stride and brilliant ability to subtly vary his pace. This brought him 1,182 wickets for Surrey in 306 appearances, at an average of 17.99. He made his Test debut in 1893, touring Australia in 1894/95 and eventually taking 43 wickets in 12 Tests.

25th MARCH 1989

Thomas Lloyd Maynard was born in Cardiff. After attending Pentyrch Primary School and Radyr Comprehensive, Maynard moved to Millfield School where he was friends with future Surrey captain Rory Hamilton-Brown. The two would play together at Surrey when Maynard joined in 2011, making an immediate impact. He scored 1,657 first-class runs for the club – including four centuries – as well as a further 898 in one-day and Twenty20 cricket before his tragic death in 2012.

26th MARCH 1985

Pat Pocock played his only one-day international for England, the Consolation Final in the Rothmans Four Nations Cup, a tournament in Sharjah, UAE, featuring England, Australia, India and Pakistan. England lost the game by 43 runs with Pocock returning a creditable 0-20 from his ten overs.

27th MARCH 2001

Graham Thorpe captained England for the last time in a one-day international against Sri Lanka in Colombo. After their glorious victory in the Test series, England had suffered two defeats in the one-day series and this was to be their third. Alec Stewart scored 14 and Thorpe a first-ball duck before Sri Lanka scored the 166 runs required in just 33.5 overs without losing a wicket.

28th MARCH 1943

Future Surrey president Sir Richard Stilgoe was born in Camberley. Stilgoe is a regular feature on television and radio and wrote the lyrics for West End musical *Starlight Express*. He served as the Surrey president in 2005.

29th MARCH 1871

Surrey and England batsman Tom Hayward was born in Cambridge. His grandfather Daniel and father, also Daniel, had played for Surrey before him and Tom made his debut for the club in 1893. From 1895 to his retirement at the outbreak of the First World War Hayward never failed to reach 1,000 runs in a season, passing 2,000 on ten occasions and – in 1904 and 1906 – scoring more than 3,000. Overall he played 593 times for Surrey, scoring 36,171 runs at an average of 42.40. Both of these achievements are second only to Sir Jack Hobbs and unlikely to ever be equalled. He made his Test debut in 1896, playing for his country 35 times and scoring 1,999 runs at 34.46. Less widely known is that he was also a proficient medium-pace bowler, taking 481 first-class wickets, including best figures of 8-89 against Warwickshire at Edgbaston in 1901. The great Neville Cardus wrote that Hayward 'was amongst the most precisely technical and most prolific batsmen of any time in the annals of cricket'.

29th MARCH 1943

Sir John Major was born in Sutton. The son of a former music hall performer and shopkeeper, Major initially left school with just three O-levels but rose to become a Conservative MP in 1979, Chancellor of the Exchequer in 1989 and Prime Minister in 1990. A lifelong fan of cricket, Major served as Surrey president from 2000–2001 and has the John Major Room in the OCS Stand named after him, a room decorated with 11 pictures of his all-time Surrey XI.

30th MARCH 2002

Mark Ramprakash began his final Test match, against New Zealand at Eden Park. Somewhat echoing his international career, the top-class batsman only scored nine and two as England lost by 78 runs.

31st MARCH 1983

Hashim Mahomed Amla was born in Durban, Natal. During South Africa's tour of England in 2012, Amla became the first man since Sir Leonard Hutton to hit a Test match triple century at The Oval, as he scored 311* in South Africa's first-innings 637/2.

SURREY CCC
On This Day

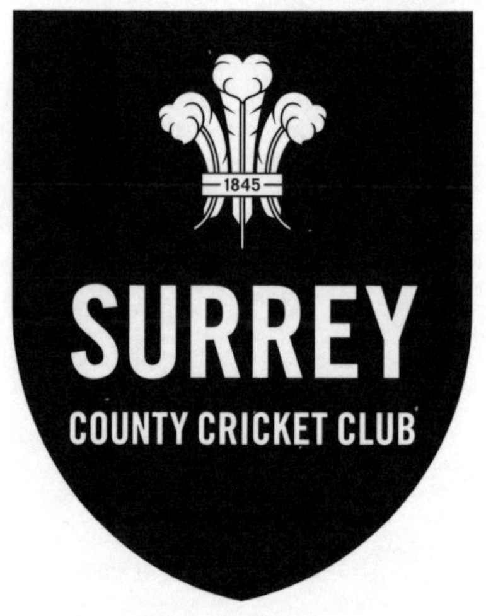

APRIL

1st APRIL 1936

George Gregory Jones was born in Mitcham. The right-arm fast bowler made his Surrey debut in 1875, taking 321 wickets at an average of 16.85. Jones's biggest claim to fame came in 1884 when – alongside 11 Surrey colleagues – he became one of the first ever players to be capped by the club.

2nd APRIL 2004

England started the second day of the third Test at the Kensington Oval on 20/1 having bowled out the West Indies for 224. Although England only secured a two-run first-innings lead, Graham Thorpe stood head and shoulders above his team-mates, scoring 119* while no other batsman scored more than 17. The innings was described on Cricinfo as 'one of his greatest'.

3rd APRIL 1930

Surrey batsman Andy Sandham started to bat his way into the history books after ending the first day of the third Test at Sabina Park, Kingston, Jamaica, on 151*. His innings on day one was an amazing feat but was eclipsed by his performance on the second day, when he once again batted from start to finish, ending on 309*. He was eventually bowled by Herman Griffith on the morning of the third day for 325, the first ever batsman to hit a Test triple century.

4th APRIL 2010

Sir Alec Bedser died in hospital in Woking, aged 91. Tributes were paid to the great bowler from across the world of cricket. His obituary in *The Guardian* began with the phrase: 'It would be hard to find a more endearingly old-fashioned, uncomplicated man – or, many would say, a finer bowler – than Sir Alec Bedser.' This point was borne out by Bedser's team-mate and fellow Surrey great Micky Stewart who recalled a time when, after Bedser had taken 11 wickets in a Test against India at Lord's in 1946, the press rang his home to get his mother's reaction to her son's feat and she replied: 'Well, isn't that what he's supposed to do as a bowler?'

5th APRIL 1989

Surrey played Hampshire in the first of two pre-season matches taking place at Sharjah in the United Arab Emirates. Hampshire had won the first encounter by virtue of losing fewer wickets but produced a more clinical victory in the second, easily topping Surrey's below-par 182 with 73 from Richard Scott.

6th APRIL 2009

The club announced that Martin Bicknell, who had not been involved at Surrey since his mid-season retirement in 2006, would be returning as the part-time bowling coach. Speaking at the time, Bicknell said: 'Coming back is something I always hoped to do. When I retired, I knew I was going to go away for a couple of years, leave the county scene completely and gain some experience. I'm a couple of years older, a bit wiser and it's my time to give a bit back to Surrey.'

7th APRIL 2010

Surrey unveiled Australian powerhouse Andrew Symonds as their overseas signing for the Friends Provident t20 competition. Despite coach Chris Adams's hopes that Symonds would provide an 'X-Factor' in the club's squad, he only managed 263 runs at 20.23 in a disappointing campaign that saw Surrey fail to reach the knockout stages.

8th APRIL 1994

Alec Stewart celebrated his 31st birthday by opening the batting for England in the fourth Test at the Kensington Oval and scoring 118. He put on 171 for the first wicket alongside captain Michael Atherton as the pair repelled the West Indian bowlers including Curtly Ambrose, Courtney Walsh and Winston and Kenny Benjamin, helping England regain face after three consecutive heavy defeats in the first three Tests of the tour.

9th APRIL 1857

Fast bowler Charles Horner was born near Dulwich Common. Horner – who was the brother-in-law of the great John Shuter – played 53 games for Surrey, taking 217 wickets at an average of 16.72. In 1884 he was among the first 12 men to receive their Surrey cap.

10th APRIL 2012

Kevin Pietersen became the first serving Surrey player to appear in the Indian Premier League, representing the Chennai Super Kings in a match in Delhi against the Delhi Daredevils. The big-hitting batsman was impressive in the match, scoring 46 from 26 balls as Chennai won by eight wickets with more than six overs remaining.

11th APRIL 1895

Caryl Thain was born in Catherington, Hampshire. Although Thain only played two first-class matches for Surrey – against Glamorgan and

Scotland in 1923, taking three wickets and scoring four runs – he served on the committee for many years, becoming first honorary treasurer and then president in 1969.

12th APRIL 1994

Not content with having hit 118 on the first day, Alec Stewart started day three of the fourth Test against the West Indies in Barbados on 62* in the second innings. Thanks to Stewart, who was eventually bowled by Courtney Walsh for 143 – and a breezy 84 from Graham Thorpe – England were able to declare on 394/7 and proceed to a famous victory on the last two days. Stewart's twin centuries made him the first Englishman to score a century in both innings against the West Indies.

13th APRIL 1992

Stuart Surridge, one of Surrey's greatest ever captains, died at Glossop, Derbyshire. Hailing from a famous family of bat manufacturers, Surridge did not play for Surrey until he was 30 but was made captain in 1952 – aged 35 – and led Surrey to the County Championship in all five of his seasons in charge. Although occasionally controversial, Surridge was ruthless in his tactics and contributed with both the ball (464 wickets at 29.64) and the bat (3,697 runs at 13.01). Further to this he was also an extremely brave close fielder. After his retirement, Surridge ran his bat-making company and was appointed president of Surrey in 1981. Following his death his widow, Betty, was also made president in 1997, when she became the first woman to hold the job. His portrait hangs in the Long Room of The Oval, next to that of his successor as captain, Peter May.

13th APRIL 2005

The start of the 2005 County Championship was a particularly wet occasion, with play only proving occasionally possible during Surrey's drawn match with Sussex at The Oval. However, the match will not be remembered for the centuries scored by Michael Yardy and Mark Ramprakash but for the unexpected onlooker who watched what play did occur from an extraordinary vantage point more than 200 feet above the ground. With the venue long known for its urban foxes, one of The Oval's vulpine tenants had climbed on to the famous gasholder that overlooks the ground when it was empty and therefore at ground level. Then, unbeknown to the fox, the massive cylinder was then filled, quickly rising to its full height and trapping the poor creature on top! Chris Adams, then captain of the opposition, spotted it on the second day and both players and supporters enjoyed watching it forlornly padding around throughout the match.

STUART SURRIDGE, ONE OF SURREY'S GREATEST EVER CAPTAINS

14th APRIL 2012

When Surrey started the day on 161/5 in their first innings against Middlesex at Lord's, they would not have expected to end it on 95/4 in their second. This was the case though as 19 wickets fell in the day and new signing Jon Lewis propelled Surrey to a position described by journalists that evening as one of 'strong favouritism' with his first five-wicket haul for the club. Captain Rory Hamilton-Brown started the day 8* in the first innings and ended it 51* in the second – but sadly was unable to lead his side to their second four-day win at Lord's in the last 18 attempts as Surrey lost in nail-biting fashion the following morning, coming up just three runs short.

15th APRIL 1999

Ian Salisbury started the 1999 season in positive fashion as he took figures of 5-44 against Gloucestershire. At the end of the second day of a soggy season opener, the visitors were on 55/2 in reply to Surrey's 342 all out, with Salisbury bowling Dominic Hewson the previous evening. He continued in a similar vein the following day, his excellent figures acting as the curtain raiser for a season where the leg-spinner would take 60 wickets at 21.91.

16th APRIL 2008

The 2008 season was not a great one for Surrey, as a side coached by Alan Butcher and led – in principle – by his son Mark but in reality by a reluctant Mark Ramprakash due to Mark's serious knee injury were relegated from the First Division of the County Championship without winning a game. Often forgotten is that it got off to an excellent start. Butcher won the toss and batted against Lancashire at The Oval and at the end of day one, Ramprakash was 102* and Butcher was 80*, with Surrey on 242/2.

17th APRIL 2004

The previous year had been superb for the man who is now Surrey's team director, Chris Adams, as he led Sussex to their first ever County Championship, and 2004 was shaping up to be no worse as he got his season off to a brilliant start, cracking 101 in his first knock of the new campaign. Sadly for Surrey fans, the innings came at The Oval and allowed Adams's then side to post a first-innings lead of nearly 200.

18th APRIL 2003

The first game of the 2003 campaign saw an exciting development for all Surrey fans as BBC London launched ball-by-ball commentary of every match for the first time, hosted by the superb Mark Church. The first ball he described saw Surrey fast bowler Alex Tudor bowling to Lancashire opener (and brother of Graeme) Alec Swann. Sadly, it wasn't a day to remember for home fans with Adam Hollioake losing the toss on a 'belter' and Lancashire recording a dominant 391/2 with hundreds from Mal Loye and Stuart Law.

18th APRIL 2007

If the 2003 campaign launched the voice of Mark Church to Surrey fans around the world, 2007 introduced them to his face as well, with Surrey's home game against Yorkshire seeing the launch of the online Surrey TV, providing highlights, interviews and features on club business for free on the Surrey website. Again, it was an inauspicious beginning with Yorkshire skipper Darren Gough winning the toss and then watching his side post 390/8 on the first day.

19th APRIL 2006

The Oval hosted its 2,000th first-class match when Surrey played Derbyshire in the County Championship. Chief executive Paul Sheldon described the day as 'another landmark in the history of this magnificent ground' but it was spoilt for home fans by Derbyshire's Ant Botha who withstood some good bowling from Azhar Mahmood to reach 100 and guide his side to 392/6 at the end of the day.

19th APRIL 2012

Kevin Pietersen became just the second Surrey player to hit a Twenty20 century when he blasted 103 off just 64 balls for the Delhi Daredevils against the Deccan Chargers in Delhi.

20th APRIL 1982

Andy Sandham died in hospital in Westminster, aged 91. One of the greatest batsmen in Surrey history was remembered by *Wisden* as: 'A wonderful servant of Surrey and as Hobbs's partner for the county for 14 years.' After an incredible playing career that saw him play 525 times for Surrey (fourth on the all-time list) and score 33,312 runs (third on the all-time list) – as well as playing 14 matches for England, becoming the first man to hit a Test triple century and becoming one of only 25 players to hit a century of first-class hundreds – Sandham continued to serve the club. He was coach from 1946 to 1958, winning seven consecutive County Championship titles, and then for the next 12 years served as scorer, working alongside a man still employed today, former head groundsman Bill Gordon.

20th APRIL 2007

Adam Hollioake, alongside his mother and father, opened the brand new Ben Hollioake Learning Centre at The Oval. The new centre, named in honour of Adam's younger brother Ben, allowed the club to deliver a Playing for Success programme for the first time, working with local schools to provide extra tuition and state-of-the-art equipment for their pupils. After performing the official opening, Adam said: 'The Ben Hollioake Learning Centre is a great facility that obviously benefits a lot of people, and will leave a great legacy to remember Ben by.'

20th APRIL 1844

Edward D'Oyley 'Ted' Barratt was born, far from Surrey, in Stockton-on-Tees, County Durham. Leg-spinner Barratt played 130 times for the club, taking 706 wickets at an average of just 17.31. A renowned bowler of the time, no less an authority than W.G. Grace wrote: 'It was rather hard luck on Barratt that when he represented Surrey the 11 was not only weak, but had very little fast bowling. In many matches he was kept on too long because there was no one good enough to relieve him, and the consequence was that the batsmen got set and hit him.' After his retirement in 1886, Barratt joined the staff at The Oval before leaving to become the landlord of the nearby Duchy Arms, where he sadly died of consumption aged just 46.

21st APRIL 1844

Edward D'Oyley 'Ted' Barratt was born in Stockton-on-Tees, County Durham. A left handed, slow, round arm bowler, Barratt made his Surrey debut in 1876 and went onto take 706 wickets for the club at just 17.31. His finest hour was taking 10/43 for the Players against Australia at The Oval in September 1878.

22nd APRIL 2001

Surrey immediately began to reap the benefits of one of the biggest 'transfers' in the history of county cricket, with Mark Ramprakash, already 51* overnight, going on to make 146 in his first innings in a Surrey shirt. He fitted seamlessly into an already strong Surrey batting order, putting on 151 with Ian Ward, 89 with Adam Hollioake and 91 with Ali Brown before finally being bowled by Kabir Ali.

23rd APRIL 1986

Jim Laker died in Putney, aged just 64, after an extraordinary career that had seen him take 1,395 wickets for Surrey (seventh on the all-time list) at just 17.37. He eventually made an excellent career commentating on TV for the BBC, where the legendary John Arlott said of him that he was

THE HOLLIOAKE FAMILY JOIN FORMER SURREY CHIEF EXECUTIVE PAUL SHELDON TO OPEN THE BEN HOLLIOAKE LEARNING CENTRE AT THE OVAL

'wry, dry, laconic; he thought about cricket with a deep intensity and a splendidly ironic point of view'.

24th APRIL 1905

The first match of Surrey's 1905 season saw a side captained by Lord Dalmeny take on the Gentlemen of England, led by W.G. Grace. Not normally a terrifically historic occasion, this game was different as it marked the first-class debut of Jack Hobbs, who opened the batting alongside Tom Hayward and scored 18 in the first innings and 88 in the second.

24th APRIL 2003

The second day of the match between Surrey and Loughborough UCCE at The Oval was a batting masterclass for the students with Surrey scoring 487 runs and recording – for only the second time in club history – four individual centuries in the same innings with Mark Ramprakash (205), Adam Hollioake (121), Jonathan Batty (123) and Martin Bicknell (103*) filling their boots.

25th APRIL 2002

Having won their opening game against Sussex by ten wickets, Surrey had travelled to Headingley to play Yorkshire brimming with confidence. After bowling out their hosts for 140 and moving to 115/0 on the first day fans were entitled to wonder how it could be better. The second day showed them exactly how as Surrey scored 395 – with 96 from Alec Stewart, 83 from Mark Butcher, 70 from Ian Ward, 65 from Mark Ramprakash and 64 from Azhar Mahmood – before Martin Bicknell and Alex Tudor both struck shortly before the close to leave Yorkshire 0/2 overnight.

26th APRIL 2012

Lee Fortis was appointed head groundsman of The Oval, replacing the previous incumbent Scott Patterson. Fortis, who had previously worked at The Oval before becoming head groundsman at the illustrious Honourable Artillery Company ground in the City of London, was the latest in a short but illustrious line including Bill Gordon, Paul Brind, his father Harry, Ted Warn, Bert Lock and Bosser Martin.

27th APRIL 1970

Robin Jackman recorded his career best one-day figures against Yorkshire in the Gillette Cup. Defending only 134, Jackman flew into the Yorkshire attack with characteristic aggression to take 7-33 from his 12 overs.

27th APRIL 2003

Surrey beat Essex by 15 runs at Chelmsford in the National League Division One. A partnership of 154 for the seventh wicket between Adam Hollioake and Azhar Mahmood – whose 98 remains Surrey's highest ever one-day score from number eight – took them to 268/8 before three wickets each for Alex Tudor and Saqlain Mushtaq saw Surrey win a tight game.

28th APRIL 1984

New Zealander Geoff Howarth became the first non-Englishman to captain Surrey when he took his side to Trent Bridge. The day started very well with Graham Monkhouse and Pat Pocock helping Surrey dismiss Nottinghamshire for 175 but ended less well when the Surrey top order – including Howarth himself who went for four – collapsed to 115/6 overnight.

28th APRIL 1996

Captain Alec Stewart won the toss and chose to bat against Hampshire in a Benson & Hedges Cup Group D encounter at The Oval. After David Ward fell early, Stewart took on the responsibility and hit a brilliant 160 – Surrey's highest ever one-day score from number three – as his side ended on 333/6 before bowling Hampshire out for 274 to secure a comfortable win.

29th APRIL 2007

Surrey smashed the previous world record for the highest ever score in a 50-over match when they hit 496/4 against Gloucestershire in a Friends Provident Trophy match at The Oval. Openers Alistair Brown (176 from 97 balls) and James Benning (152 from 134) started the rout, hitting 12 sixes and 35 fours between them, with a partnership of 294 for the first wicket before Rikki Clarke (82 including 72 in sixes and fours) and Jonathan Batty (29 from ten balls) provided the impetus for the rest of the innings. Gloucestershire were only able to make 239 in reply and slipped to defeat by 257 runs.

30th APRIL 1995

Surrey completed a famous victory over Gloucestershire at The Oval, one of only four occasions when a win has been achieved after being asked to follow on. The game started poorly as Surrey conceded 392 in the first innings, with Gloucestershire debutant Andrew Symonds hitting 161*. After being dismissed for 217 in the first innings, Surrey followed on and were inspired by Alistair Brown's 187 as they reached 475 early on the final day. This left Gloucestershire needing 301 to win. They never got close as Joey Benjamin, Mark Kenlock, Richard Nowell and Nadeem Shahid all took wickets as Surrey recorded a 93-run win.

SURREY CCC
On This Day

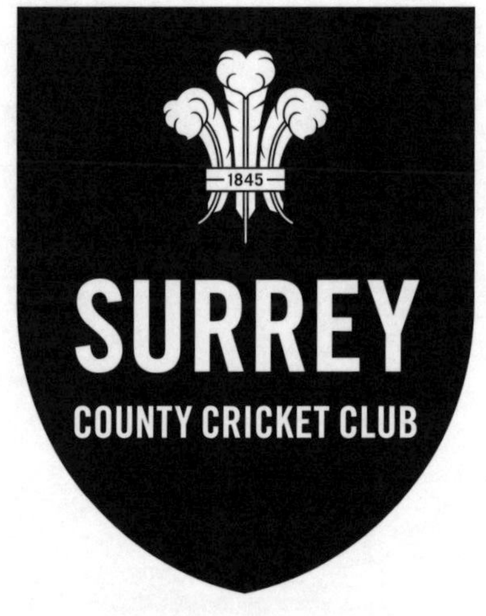

MAY

1st MAY 1936

Fast bowler David Gibson was born in Mitcham. Gibson originally represented the Army in the Inter Service competition but made his Surrey debut in 1957 at Woodbridge Road, Guildford and retained his place in the side, winning the County Championship in 1957 and 1958. He represented Surrey 185 times, taking 552 wickets at 22.22. After his retirement he became Surrey coach. In retirement he was a popular school master before emigrating to Australia, where he settled in Bowral and became a volunteer guide at the Sir Donald Bradman Museum. Gibson died in June 2012.

2nd MAY 1997

In the aftermath of one of the heaviest electoral defeats ever seen in the United Kingdom, Prime Minister John Major made his official statement of resignation, shortly before going to see the Queen for the final time. He ended by saying: 'After that I hope that Norma and I will be able, with the children, to get to The Oval in time for lunch and for some cricket this afternoon. Thank you all very much indeed.' True to his word, Major made his way from Buckingham Palace to watch Surrey's Benson & Hedges Cup fixture against British Universities. The game should have given him solace from his troubles, as Surrey – under the leadership of Ben Hollioake for the first and only time – recorded a six-wicket victory thanks to an unbeaten 86 by Sir John's favourite player, Alec Stewart.

3rd MAY 1912

Fast bowler Eddie Watts was born in Peckham. Primarily a seamer but also a more than useful right-handed batsman, Watts – the brother-in-law of Alf Gover – made his debut for Surrey in 1933 and played 240 times in total. He took 722 wickets at 25.97 and also made 6,005 runs at an average of 21.29. Another of a fine generation of Surrey men who lost six of their best years to the Second World War, Watts's finest hour came at Edgbaston on 22 August 1939 – just ten days before the outbreak of hostilities – when he took all ten wickets to fall in the Warwickshire second innings, returning figures of 10-67 and becoming the third Surrey bowler to achieve the feat.

4th MAY 1969

Surrey played their only ever match at Sutton CC, a John Player League clash against Derbyshire. The away side batted first and were dismissed for 150, leaving John Edrich to lead Surrey to a six-wicket win with an unbeaten 56.

4th MAY 1990

Surrey had begun a remarkable game against Lancashire by batting all day to reach 396/6. It was on day two when the match started to show its true colours. Keith Medlycott was dismissed early on, leaving the way clear for Martin Bicknell and skipper Ian Greig to put on 205 for the eighth wicket, still a club record. When Bicknell went, Neil Kendrick picked up his mantle and added another 101 for the ninth wicket, the partnership only broken when Greig went for 291, nine short of his triple century, and Surrey declared on 707/9. Amazingly, that wasn't even the highest score of the match as, buoyed by a partnership of 364 between Neil Fairbrother (366) and a young Michael Atherton (191), Lancashire posted 863 all out – the highest score ever posted against Surrey and second-highest ever at The Oval. Less surprisingly, the match ended in a draw.

5th MAY 1905

Jack Hobbs hit the first of what would go on to become 199 first-class centuries in the match against Essex at The Oval. With Surrey needing a big score to give their bowlers something to attack, Hobbs scored 158 and with fifties from Albert Baker and Ernest Nice, helped his side to 383 and an eventual 185-run victory.

5th MAY 1953

Opening batsman Grahame Clinton was born in Sidcup. After signing from Kent ahead of the 1979 season, Clinton played 234 games for Surrey, scoring 11,838 runs at an average of 34.61 and forming an opening partnership with Alan Butcher that would characterise the club throughout the first half of the 1980s, although he once added 321 for the first wicket alongside Darren Bicknell in his final season of 1990. Appropriately, his final innings before retirement, in September 1990, was against his former county of Kent. He was later Surrey's second XI coach and batting coach.

6th MAY 1909

Surrey ended the first day of their County Championship match against Hampshire on 654/4, despite the loss of Tom Hayward early on for just 33. He was replaced at the crease by Ernie Hayes, who partnered Jack Hobbs to put on 371 for the second wicket, a club record that still stands. Hayes's 276 was a career best while Hobbs managed 'just' 205.

6th MAY 1953

The second match of the 1953 season saw Surrey play MCC at Lord's and stand-in captain Peter May decided to give a first-class debut to promising youngster Ken Barrington. There was little sign of what was to come though – either in Barrington's career or the rest of the season – with Barrington making eight in the first innings and 17 in the second and Surrey losing by 107 runs.

6th MAY 1964

Surrey travelled to the Ellerman Line Sports Club in Hoylake to play Cheshire in the first round of the Gillette Cup – only the second one-day match the club had played after being knocked out in the first round the previous year. Although they only managed 171/8 from their 60 overs (thanks to 70 from John Edrich), the first Surrey one-day hat-trick from David Sydenham saw them to a 62-run victory.

7th MAY 1886

John William 'Bill' Hitch was born in Radcliffe, Lancashire. The hugely popular fast bowler – a Lancastrian by birth – was spotted playing for a club in Cambridgeshire by Tom Hayward and recommended to The Oval, where he made his debut for Surrey against Hampshire in 1907. He would play 305 times and take a magnificent haul of 1,232 wickets at 21.55. He also blasted 6,765 runs in an uncomplicated style that endeared him to many Surrey fans. His highest first-class score, 107 against Somerset in Bath, took just 70 minutes. Although undoubtedly one of the finest county bowlers of his age, he only played seven Tests, taking just seven wickets but hitting 51* against Australia in front of his home crowd in his final match in 1921.

8th MAY 1948

Australia played the fourth game of Don Bradman's final tour, against Surrey at The Oval, and ended the first day 479/4, with Bradman scoring 146. However, it wasn't Bradman or fellow centurions Sid Barnes or Lindsay Hassett who went down in the record books but Surrey left-arm spinner John McMahon whose 42.2 overs went for 210 runs. This remains a club record and one of only two occasions when a Surrey bowler has conceded more than 200 in an innings.

8th MAY 1963

Surrey played Derbyshire in the County Championship and decided to give young pace bowler Geoff Arnold his first-class debut. After Micky Stewart won the toss and opted to bat, Arnold had a quiet day, not batting when Surrey declared on 343/7 and then indulging in a spot of mild celebration when David Gibson and Peter Loader took wickets before the close to leave Derbyshire on 4/2 overnight.

9th MAY 1993

Surrey played their first game in coloured clothing, against Sussex at Hove. Chasing 304 to win, Alec Stewart's side came up short at 245 all out despite 73 from David Ward and 54 from Monte Lynch.

10th MAY 1987

Gordon Greenidge smashed 172 against Surrey in a Refuge Assurance League match at Southampton. His innings was even worse for the fielders as Ian Greig had won the toss and asked his opposite number – Mark Nicholas – to bat first. Greenidge's total remains the second-highest individual score against Surrey in a one-day match and the highest by an opener.

11th MAY 1904

Legendary off-spinner William 'Razor' Smith took his career best figures of 9-31 for Surrey against Hampshire in a County Championship match at The Oval. The only blot on the innings was Hampshire wicketkeeper Jimmy Stone, who was inconveniently caught behind by Bert Strudwick off the bowling of Robert Sheppard. Surrey, who were already well on top, completed a 253-run victory.

11th MAY 1946

Surrey had reduced India to 205/9 at The Oval and would have been confident of bowling them out for a manageable total. However, Chandra Sarwate and Shute Banerjee had different ideas. The pair withstood a Surrey attack including Alf Gover, Alec Bedser and Eddie Watts to put on 249 for the final wicket, an effort that is still the second-highest tenth-wicket partnership ever. However, the Surrey players walked off with spirits still high, as the match was the first full day of cricket played at The Oval since 15th August 1939.

11th MAY 1948

Having allowed Australia to reach 632 in their first innings, Surrey were unlikely to record a victory against Bradman's men. A first innings of just 141 made such a result even less likely. Following on, their second effort of 195 was marginally better but still meant they equalled the club's worst defeat ever – against England in 1866 – by an innings and 296 runs.

11th MAY 2008

Young paceman Jade Dernbach became the first Surrey bowler ever to concede more than 100 runs in a one-day game when he recorded figures of 0-107 from his ten overs against Essex at The Oval.

12th MAY 1965

Keith Thomas Medlycott was born in Whitechapel. Although 'Medders' was a fine player for Surrey, playing 134 times and averaging 26.36 with the bat and 32.40 with the ball it is as a coach he will be largely remembered, teaming with Adam Hollioake to lift three County Championships and four one-day trophies during his time at the helm, from 1998 until 2003.

13th MAY 1845

Montpelier CC played a one-day match with a dinner staged afterwards to discuss the potential formation of a Surrey County Cricket Club. The proposal was for the new side to play at a market garden in Kennington – owned by the Duchy of Cornwall – for which club officials had recently secured a lease allowing its conversion into a cricket ground.

13th MAY 1872

Surrey dismissed MCC for just 16 during a match at Lord's, the lowest ever total scored against the club. The wickets were shared between James Southerton (4-5) and William Marten (6-11).

14th MAY 1918

Arthur John William McIntyre was born in Kennington, within a quarter-mile of The Oval. He made his debut in 1938, as a leg-spinning all-rounder, before heading off to war, where he was injured in the Anzio Landings of 1944. Post-war he successfully filled in at wicketkeeper and took on the position full-time after the retirement of Gerald Mobey. He would go on to play a vital role in all seven County Championship victories achieved from 1952 to 1958 but, due to the prominence of Godfrey Evans, only played three Tests. After his death in 2009, his *Daily Telegraph* obituary observed: 'McIntyre was unfortunate in that the panache and brilliance behind the stumps of Godfrey Evans, who was two years younger, prevented him playing more than three times for England. Many good judges, however, felt that there was little to choose between the two wicketkeepers.'

15th MAY 2007

Surrey announced that, in honour of their long standing association, they had named a room in the new OCS Stand as the John Major Room. Chief executive Paul Sheldon observed: 'Sir John was a wonderful ambassador for Surrey and we are proud to be able to honour his continued association with the club.'

16th MAY 1956

One of the greatest feats in cricket, often mentioned when listing superlatives, is Jim Laker's ten-wicket haul against Australia at Old Trafford in 1956. What is less well known however is the fact that Laker had already achieved the feat against the same opponents that summer. Eight of the side that would go on to to play in Manchester played against Surrey at The Oval, with Laker bowling superbly all day to single-handedly bowl the side out for 259. He finished on 10-88 with Surrey progressing to 34/0 by the close, David Fletcher (15*) and Tom Clark (18*) the not out men.

16th MAY 2010

England won their first piece of silverware at a World Cup of any format when they claimed the ICC World T20 in the West Indies. Surrey were well represented on the field by future players Kevin Pietersen and Dirk Nannes, plus Australian all-rounder Steve Smith, who played five games for the second XI back in 2007.

17th MAY 1794

John Bayley was born in Mitcham, the only player to have been born in the 18th century and still play for Surrey. Already an established cricketer, Bayley was 56 when he played against Kent at The Oval in 1846. He batted at number 11 and did not bowl but fared slightly better when the two sides played again at Aylesford a month later, scoring ten runs and taking a wicket.

18th MAY 1991

Surrey started a first-class friendly against Cambridge University at Fenner's in which Keith Medlycott achieved the unusual and impressive feat of scoring 100 runs and taking more than ten wickets in the same match. Although he only managed two in the first innings, 109 in the second – coupled with 5-36 and 6-98 – meant Medlycott became the sixth man to do so for Surrey.

19th MAY 2011

In a spectacle none of the attendant crowd – nor possibly the Surrey players – will ever forget, Graham Napier utilised the unforgiving short boundaries at Whitgift School to equal the record for the number of sixes in a first-class innings, 16. He was eventually caught behind off Stuart Meaker for a brutal 196 from 130 deliveries.

20th MAY 1958

Peter Loader took his career best figures of 9-17 as Surrey beat Warwickshire by an innings and 80 runs at The Oval.

20th MAY 1973

Surrey played their only match at the Decca Sports Ground in Tolworth. Under the leadership of John Edrich they lost to Northamptonshire by 12 runs.

20th MAY 2009

Veteran all-rounder Chris Lewis, a left-field selection by Alan Butcher for the 2008 Twenty20 campaign, eight years after he had last played a first-class game, was sentenced to 13 years in jail after being caught trying to smuggle cocaine worth more than £140,000 through Gatwick Airport. He had been attempting to conceal the drug in tins of pineapple and grapefruit juice hidden in his cricket bag. On the same day there were happier scenes at The Oval with Scott Newman hitting 177 in a Friends Provident match against Yorkshire, his one-day best and the fourth-highest one-day innings in club history.

21st MAY 1885

Since 27th July 1865, there had been a special rivalry between Surrey fans and their counterparts north of the river who supported Middlesex. While the modern concept of 'fandom' was probably in its infancy in 1885, it nonetheless would have been a satisfying time for Surrey supporters as John Beaumont and George Lohmann combined to bowl Middlesex out for a record low score of 25 at Lord's. Surrey went on to win by an innings and 64 runs – a decent feat when they only scored 166 themselves!

22nd MAY 1963

Surrey travelled to New Road, Worcester, to play Worcestershire in the nascent Gillette Cup, the country's first one-day tournament. As the competition format was a straight knockout, the club's experiment with limited overs cricket did not last long as they were defeated by 114 runs.

22nd MAY 1999

The Oval staged its first game in the 1999 Cricket World Cup, with South Africa beating England by 122 runs in a low scoring encounter lit up by Alan Donald's brilliant 4-17 from eight overs.

23rd MAY 1917

Lance Corporal Henry Blacklidge, who had played seven first-class games for Surrey between 1908 and May 1913, was killed at Amara in Mesopotamia. Henry had taken seven wickets for Surrey and scored exactly 100 runs. His body is buried in the Amara War Cemetery.

23rd MAY 1918

Denis Compton was born in Hendon, Middlesex. Although a legend of Surrey's most bitter rivals, Compton also holds the distinguished achievement of having played the most Test matches at The Oval, appearing in 13 games between his debut – at the same ground in 1937 – and his final Test in Kennington in 1956.

23rd MAY 1946

Surrey, captained by Nigel Bennett, played an Old England XI, led by Percy Fender, in a match to celebrate the centenary of Surrey CCC. The celebrations had been delayed a year by the Second World War and the match – umpired by Jack Hobbs and Bert Strudwick – was drawn with Surrey scoring 248/6 and England 232/5.

24th MAY 1947

Surrey's County Championship match with Nottinghamshire at Trent Bridge began. When Nottinghamshire reached the end of the day on 366/8 there was no indication the game would contain any special achievements. However, Surrey ended day two 443/2 with David Fletcher and Stan Squires already having made centuries. When John Parker and skipper Errol Holmes both joined them on three figures during the final day it became the first game in which Surrey players had scored four individual centuries in the same innings.

25th MAY 1846

Surrey's game played against MCC was listed as the maiden 'first-class' match to be played by the club at The Oval. Twenty-seven wickets fell on the first day of the game with MCC bowled out for 57, Surrey for 37 and MCC ending on 63/7.

25th MAY 1997

Ben Hollioake made his England debut in the third Texaco Trophy one-day international against Australia at Lord's. The precocious all-rounder got off the mark by straight-driving Glenn McGrath back down the ground to the Pavilion End and then continued to blaze one of the finest attacks in the modern game all over the Home of Cricket, hitting 63 in just over an hour as England won by six wickets.

25th MAY 2009

Mark Ramprakash and Usman Afzaal put on an unbroken stand of 139 for the second wicket during a Twenty20 game against Middlesex at Lord's. The stand remains the highest in club history and helped Surrey record a 57-run victory.

26th MAY 2011

Surrey announced the signing of Dirk Nannes as their overseas player for the 2011 Twenty20 season. Nannes, a very quick left-arm seamer, was the leading wicket-taker in the history of Twenty20 cricket having previously claimed 134 victims. He ended the year with 19 more at 20.05.

27th MAY 1964

The Oval staged its first limited overs match as Surrey took on Gloucestershire in the Gillette Cup. Seeking revenge for their loss in the previous year's competition, Surrey had 96 from Man of the Match John Edrich to thank for their 268/6 from 60 overs before slow left-armer Roger Harman took 3-50 as Surrey won by 46 runs.

27th MAY 1998

Saqlain Mushtaq took a hat-trick in the Benson & Hedges Cup quarter-final against Lancashire in his 4-46 at The Oval. Once the game had been extended into the second day due to inclement weather, Surrey comfortably advanced to the semi-finals, winning by five wickets.

27th MAY 2004

Surrey wicketkeeper Jonathan Batty took eight catches in the same innings during a County Championship game against Kent at The Oval. The achievement meant Batty joined an elite group of eight other wicketkeepers to have completed the feat, with his brilliant performance underlined by the 129 he had scored in the first innings, Surrey's seven-wicket victory and the fact he was captaining the side.

28th MAY 1916

Lieutenant Harry Chinnery was killed in Monchy-le-Preux, France. Chinnery had played 66 first-class games for Surrey from 1897 to 1910, scoring 2,536 runs at 24.86. He was buried in the Berles-au-Bois Churchyard Extension near Arras in Northern France.

SURREY GREATS JACK HOBBS AND HERBERT STRUDWICK UMPIRE A MATCH BETWEEN SURREY AND OLD ENGLAND AT THE OVAL TO CELEBRATE THE CLUB'S CENTENARY

28th MAY 1972

Surrey played their only game at the picturesque Charterhouse School, a John Player League clash with Warwickshire. The rain-affected match was won by the visitors on a faster scoring rate, securing the full four points.

29th MAY 1899

Captain Kingsmill Key won the toss against Somerset at The Oval and decided to bat. His decision paid off handsomely as the great 'Guvnor' Bobby Abel proved impregnable all day, ending 227* with Surrey on 495/5. Abel continued his innings long into the second day, eventually concluding his knock on 357* when Surrey were bowled out for 811. The total remains the club's highest ever score in a single innings and the subsequent margin of victory – an innings and 379 runs – the third-largest by Surrey.

29th MAY 1999

Adam Hollioake played his last game of one-day international cricket, against India at Edgbaston in the World Cup. Another Surrey player who never quite fulfilled his international pedigree, Hollioake scored just six runs and bowled five wicketless overs. However, in future years England's loss was very much Surrey's gain.

30th MAY 1946

Robert George Dylan 'Bob' Willis was born in Sunderland, County Durham. After having moved to the Surrey village of Stoke d'Abernon aged six, Willis came through the Surrey youth system and made his debut in August 1969. He only played 34 games for Surrey though, moving to Warwickshire ahead of the 1972 season – although he did make his Test debut whilst a Surrey player, playing at the Sydney Cricket Ground in January 1971.

30th MAY 1983

In an extraordinary day's cricket at Chelmsford, Surrey recorded their lowest ever first-class score when a side led by Roger Knight was dismissed for just 14 against Essex. Grahame Clinton had the dubious honour of being the top scorer – with six – as seven Surrey players made ducks. The only other run scorers were Alan Butcher (2), Graham Monkhouse (2) and Sylvester Clarke (4).

31st MAY 1847

Surrey played MCC in their first game at Lord's Cricket Ground, which they sadly lost by four wickets. MCC won the toss and batted first, scoring 148 in their first innings. Surrey then replied but fell exactly 100 short as they were skittled out for just 48 to end the first day. Asked to follow on they faired considerably better on the second day, reaching 192 thanks to 82 from Nicholas 'Felix' Wanostrocht, a noted amateur cricketer of the time. MCC were left requiring 92 to win and when they were 67/6, Surrey may have hoped they could steal an unlikely victory. However, Robert Grinston and Samuel Dakin were the saviours of the home side, combining for the remaining 25 runs to give MCC a four-wicket success. The match was the first of many hotly contested encounters between Surrey and MCC over the forthcoming years.

31st MAY 1927

Baron Michael Sandberg was born in Surrey. He decided to join the Army in 1945 and then volunteered to join the Indian Army. Upon Indian independence he rejoined the British Army and joined the First King's Dragoon Guards. In 1949 he left the Army and joined the Hong Kong & Shanghai Banking Corporation where he rose through the ranks and was appointed chairman and chief executive in 1977. While at HSBC he was responsible for the building of the landmark HSBC Main Building in central Hong Kong, at the time the most expensive building in the world. He was knighted on his retirement from the bank in 1986 and was appointed Surrey president for a year in 1988. He embarked on a second career in 1997 when he was made a Life Peer and now sits in the House of Lords.

31st MAY 1998

Surrey completed an innings victory over Kent at The Oval. The visitors had been dismissed for just 86 in their first innings and although they made a better fist of their second, they still lost by an innings and 30 runs. The most notable achievement in the match was by Graham Thorpe, who took six catches in the Kent first innings – just one short of the world record of seven.

SURREY CCC
On This Day

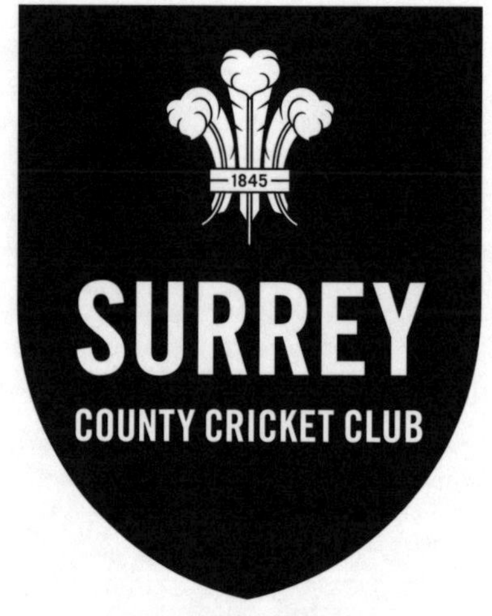

JUNE

1st JUNE 1911

Walter Lees started his final game of first-class cricket, a County Championship match at The Oval against Sussex. He took 1-6 in the first innings and 0-51 in the second, ending his career with 1,402 wickets at a superb average of 21.40.

1st JUNE 2011

When Jade Dernbach was called up to provide cover for the England Test squad at Lord's, 19-year-old bowler Matthew Dunn was thrown in to the Surrey side to make his County Championship debut against Derbyshire at Derby. Having taken two wickets the previous evening, Dunn continued his brilliant start, removing three more to secure 5-56 and leave his side just 142 to win, which was knocked off in thrilling style.

2nd JUNE 1865

Future Surrey and England great George Lohmann was born in Kensington. Lohmann is commonly regarded as one of the greatest bowlers of all time and boasts the lowest Test average of any bowler to have taken more than 15 wickets, 10.75. He is also the second on the list of the ICC all-time bowlers ranking, behind just Sydney Barnes. Lohmann, who bowled medium pace but with an uncanny knack to spin the ball viciously, made his Surrey debut in 1884 and played for the club until 1896, taking 1,221 wickets at 13.19 in just 186 appearances. He was also an accomplished batsman and scored 5,070 runs for Surrey, including two centuries. Lohmann made his Test debut at Old Trafford in 1886 and played 18 Tests before his last at Lord's in 1896, taking 112 wickets. His career was sadly dogged by tuberculosis which he contracted in 1892, with Lohmann splitting his time between England and South Africa for health reasons before eventually emigrating for good in 1897 and dying, tragically young, at the age of 36 in 1901.

3rd JUNE 1878

Surrey started their first ever tour match, against Australia at The Oval. An eventful first day saw Surrey all out for 107 and Australia also all out for 110. After Surrey managed just 80 in the second innings, they eventually fell to a five-wicket defeat.

4th JUNE 1998

Saqlain Mushtaq bowled the first of the 60 overs he would put down against Worcestershire at The Oval. The Pakistani spinner's efforts saw him equal the modern club record of 360 individual deliveries in an innings by Eric Bedser in 1958.

5th JUNE 1921

Playing Essex at the County Ground in Leyton, Surrey had bowled their hosts out for 104 – with five wickets each for Tom Jennings and Percy Fender – but were in danger of not fully capitalising when they ended the day 307/9. However, the start of the second day must rank as one of the most frustrating in Essex's history with Andy Ducat (290*) being joined by Andrew Sandham, batting out of place at number 11, to add a club record 173 for the last wicket.

5th JUNE 1997

Mark Butcher made his Test debut at Edgbaston on the grand occasion of a home England Ashes victory in the 1990s. When Mark Taylor won the toss and chose to bat, Butcher would have been forgiven for assuming he would not bat until later in the game but Andrew Caddick inspired England to bowl out Taylor's men for 118. Butcher only managed eight before being caught behind by Ian Healy off Michael Kasprowicz but it had been a superb day for England who ended on 478/9 and went on to win by nine wickets.

5th JUNE 2005

Graham Thorpe joined Alec Stewart as the only Surrey players to play a century of Tests when he started his 100th – and final one – against Bangladesh at Chester-le-Street. Thorpe's last contribution was an unbeaten 66 and catching Anwar Hossain Monir off Matthew Hoggard as England won by an innings and 27 runs.

6th JUNE 1868

Surrey completed a tied match with MCC at The Oval – just one of six in club history. With 94 the target in the second innings, Tom Sewell was caught by a substitute fielder off the bowling of W.G. Grace's brother Edward to leave his side 93 all out.

6th JUNE 1907

George Richard Hodges Nugent, Baron Nugent of Guildford and president of Surrey from 1965 to 1968, was born. In his role as president of the Royal Society for the Prevention of Accidents, he was credited with introducing legislation to make the wearing of a seatbelt in a car compulsory in 1981.

6th JUNE 1963

The great John Edrich made his Test debut against the West Indies at Old Trafford. The opening day was quiet for him though, as the West Indies batted first and moved to 244/3 at stumps. He eventually played his first innings the next evening, part of an all-Surrey top order as he opened alongside Micky Stewart with Ken Barrington at number three.

6th JUNE 1990

Pakistani quick bowler Waqar Younis made his Surrey debut, against Derbyshire at The Oval. Thought of at the time as one of the most exciting young talents in world cricket, the 19-year-old did not disappoint, taking 4-77 in a match that was eventually ruined by rain.

6th JUNE 1991

Mark Ramprakash made his Test debut against the West Indies at Headingley. Already considered one of the most promising English batsmen of his generation, Ramprakash scored two innings of 27 as England secured a crucial 115-run victory. His 52nd and final cap came in 2002 while a Surrey player.

6th JUNE 2007

Surrey endured a thankless day in the field against Worcestershire at New Road with first Phil Jacques (124), Stephen Moore (143) and Vikram Solanki (232) putting their bowling to the sword. Worcestershire declared on the second afternoon with 701/6, only the fourth time Surrey had conceded over 700 in an innings.

6th JUNE 2009

The Oval hosted its first two matches in the ICC World T20, New Zealand vs. Scotland and Australia vs. West Indies. Chris Gayle, again, peppered the roads of Kennington with a series of huge hits.

7th JUNE 1957

Micky Stewart equalled the world record as he took seven catches in one innings during Surrey's ten-wicket win over Northamptonshire at the County Ground, Northampton. At the time he was the first man to achieve the feat and it has only been equalled twice – by Gloucestershire's Tony Brown in 1966 and Warwickshire's Rikki Clarke in 2011.

7th JUNE 1986

Martin Bicknell made his Surrey debut against Derbyshire at The Oval. Bowling as part of an attack that also included Sylvester Clarke and Pat Pocock, Bicknell took 2-23 in the first innings and then 3-30 in the second as Surrey won by nine wickets.

8th JUNE 1951

So often the forgotten twin, Eric Bedser took this chance to shine when Alec was away playing in the first Test. In the first innings of Surrey's match against Gloucestershire at The Oval, Bedser took 7-142 and then immediately backed this up with an innings of 71 as he opened the batting. After another three wickets in the second innings and a further knock of 30, Eric became one of only six men to score 100 runs and take ten wickets in the same match for Surrey.

8th JUNE 2006

Surrey started day two of their County Championship match with Leicestershire at The Oval on 64/1. By the end of the day they were 416/4 and motoring. They would carry on to make 668/7 declared, with a double century from Alistair Brown and hundreds from Mark Butcher and Rikki Clarke. During the innings, Leicestershire bowler Claude Henderson achieved the dubious distinction of conceding the most runs ever in an innings against Surrey, a massive 235 from his 54.2 overs.

9th JUNE 1955

Ken Barrington made his Test debut against South Africa at Trent Bridge. It was a very poor start for the man who would go on to become one of the greatest though, lasting just three balls before being caught by John Waite off the bowling of Eddie Fuller for a duck.

9th JUNE 1983

The Oval staged its first match of the World Cup, a 106-run victory for England over New Zealand. Man of the Match Allan Lamb hit 102 from 105 balls in England's 322/6 which New Zealand were never in with a hope of catching.

9th JUNE 2012

Mark Ramprakash walked off a cricket field for the last time following Surrey's ten-wicket defeat to Sussex at Horsham. He announced his retirement a month later during a press conference at The Oval and then appeared on the pitch during a T20 match that night to say a final farewell to the Surrey fans.

10th JUNE 1957

Tony Lock took 7-49 as Surrey claimed 14 Nottinghamshire wickets in one day at Trent Bridge. Having posted 303/4 declared, Lock starred in the first innings before returning in the second as Nottinghamshire were left hanging at 39/4 overnight. Surrey eventually won by an innings and 119 runs with Jim Laker taking 7/16 in the second innings.

10th JUNE 1999

Mark Butcher started the day 49* after his Surrey side had bowled Leicestershire out for 272 on day one at Grace Road. Butcher proceeded to bat all day, putting on 189 for the first wicket alongside Ian Ward and then taking over. No other Surrey batsman passed 30 as Butcher went relentlessly on, reaching the close at 253*. He would add a further six on the third morning before being dismissed for his highest career first-class score.

11th JUNE 1917

Lieutenant John Raphael died of his wounds at the Battle of Messines. Raphael had played 39 times for Surrey, scoring 1,614 runs at 28.31 from 1904 to 1913. He was also capped nine times for England at rugby union and captained the British Lions on tour to Argentina in 1910, playing at centre, wing and full-back. Born in Brussels in 1882, Raphael died fighting in the country of his birth and is buried at the Lijssenthoek Military Cemetery.

11th JUNE 1937

In the first innings of their County Championship match against Somerset at The Oval, Surrey made 406 with hundreds from Bob Gregory and Stan Squires. With a lead of 142, skipper Donald Knight and Andrew Sandham walked out to start the second innings but 13.4 overs later it was all over: Surrey had been dismissed for 35. Even more amazingly, the day ended with Somerset bowled out for 166 – Alf Gover taking 5-48 – and Surrey winning the match by 11 runs.

11th JUNE 1972

Surrey played their first match at Kenton Court Meadow in Sunbury, a John Player League game against Gloucestershire. After dismissing the visitors for 133, an unbroken partnership of 108 between Micky Stewart and Younis Ahmed was enough to give Surrey a nine-wicket win on run rate.

11th JUNE 1975

The Oval staged its first World Cup match as Australia beat Sri Lanka by 52 runs. Australian opener Alan Turner hit 101 of his side's 328 and Sri Lanka could only respond with 276/4. Chasing such a large target, their task was already hard enough without the mighty Jeff Thomson injuring both Sunil Wettimuny and Duleep Mendis to the extent they ended up in nearby St. Thomas' Hospital. It is alleged that, after striking Wettimuny on the foot and causing him to cry out in pain, Thomson walked down the wicket and said: 'Look, it's not broken, you weak bastard. But if you're down there the next over, it will be.' True to his word, the fastest bowler in the world returned for next over, rammed down another yorker and did indeed break the Sri Lankan's foot. However, instead of checking on his fallen opponent – and egged on by his team-mates – Thomson threw down the stumps and appealed for a run-out. 'No other bastard moved,' Thomson later said. 'They all sat or stood there with their arms folded. They'd done me stone cold!' Back at the hospital, Mendis – who had been struck on the head and concussed – was asked by a policeman who had caused his injury. 'Thomson,' he replied. Clearly unaware of the situation, the dutiful officer replied: 'Sir, do you want to press charges against this man?'

11th JUNE 1999

The Oval witnessed its first international hat-trick when Surrey legend Saqlain Mushtaq dismissed Henry Olonga, Adam Huckle and Pommie Mbangwa in successive deliveries at the end of Pakistan's World Cup group game with Zimbabwe.

12th JUNE 2002

Surrey's acting captain Ian Ward won the toss and, unusually, chose to field first against Kent at The Oval. His aggressive decision paid off handsomely as Martin Bicknell ripped through the visitors' batting order, taking 6-42. However, the difficult batting conditions were underlined by Surrey ending the day on 111/5. Eventually a superb 188 from Ali Brown was the difference between the two sides as Surrey won by nine wickets.

13th JUNE 1979

The Oval was due to stage its first game in the 1979 World Cup, between Sri Lanka and the West Indies, but – after three days of consistent rain – the game was abandoned without a ball being bowled.

13th JUNE 2003

Surrey played their first Twenty20 match, against Middlesex at The Oval, in front of a curious crowd of 10,000 – which was well over projections made by the club and caused early carnage at the bar! No one quite knew what to expect, a feeling summed up by Adam Hollioake when he won the toss and chose to bowl because: 'I haven't got a clue what's going to happen.' Three hours later, Surrey won the game by four wickets with Jimmy Ormond capturing five victims and Ian Ward leading a team effort with the bat.

14th JUNE 2003

The very next day Surrey continued their Twenty20 campaign as they played their first ever game at the Imber Court ground in East Molesey. It was another triumph, Surrey beating Essex – who were playing their first T20 match – by 44 runs, as Graham Thorpe became the first Surrey player to hit a T20 fifty and one of the format's early masters, Azhar Mahmood, took 4-20 and also hit 43 from just 18 balls.

15th JUNE 1985

Surrey and England legend Percy Fender died in Exeter aged 92. Fender started his career at Sussex but moved to Surrey at the start of the 1914 season as he wanted to combine playing cricket with a business career. He was a huge success in his first season, taking a hat-trick in his second game and scoring a hundred in his fifth with *Wisden* commenting: 'As a match winning factor he is a far greater force on a side than his records would suggest.' As soon as war was declared, Fender joined the Army, serving in the Royal Flying Corps to repel Zeppelin attacks from London. However, a broken leg playing football in 1918 saw him miss the entire 1919 season. He was appointed Surrey captain in 1920 and made his Test debut in 1921. However, an often controversial relationship with MCC authority figures meant he never progressed to captain his country, as many thought he should. He was hugely successful throughout the 1920s but was replaced as club captain by Douglas Jardine in 1931. He continued playing in the 1930s but his appearances were limited due to his other commitments and his last game for Surrey was against Middlesex at Lord's in 1935. In retirement he again served in the RAF, being mentioned in dispatches for his role preparing for the Allied Invasion of Europe. Although he went blind in the late 1970s he still travelled to Australia for the celebrations to mark the 100th anniversary of Test cricket – and was the oldest man in attendance.

16th JUNE 1948

Peter May made his first-class debut for the Combined Services at the Officer's Club Services Ground in Aldershot. It was a quiet day for May who stood in the field for Hampshire's 269 all out. He went on to make three and two as his side suffered an innings defeat.

16th JUNE 1996

In the AXA Equity and Law Sunday League at The Oval, Surrey bowled out Leicestershire for just 48 – at the time the lowest score ever made against the club. The 12 extras conceded by Surrey were the top score in the innings by four runs and, unsurprisingly, Surrey went on to win by ten wickets.

17th JUNE 1986

Future Surrey wicketkeeper-batsman Steven Davies was born in Bromsgrove, Worcestershire. After starting his career at Worcestershire, he opted to move to Surrey at the end of the 2009 season, alongside his friend and team-mate Gareth Batty. He made his England debut in October 2009 and went on to tour Australia in 2010/11, acting as cover for Matt Prior and playing in the one-day internationals and Twenty20 series.

18th JUNE 1894

Fast bowler Tom Richardson became the first man to take all ten wickets in an innings for Surrey when he powered through the Essex side who had come to The Oval for a first-class match. Only two Essex players made double figures as Richardson walked off with figures of 10-45, having bowled unchanged throughout the innings.

18th JUNE 1916

Captain Francis Gillespie was killed at Ypres in Belgium. The left-handed batsman had played six games for Surrey in the 1913 season, scoring 249 runs at an average of 22.63. Captain Gillespie, who served with the Royal Sussex Regiment, was buried at the Merville Communal Cemetery in France.

18th JUNE 1958

Douglas Jardine died in Montreux, Switzerland, where he had travelled to receive medical treatment for lung cancer. Jardine played for Surrey from 1921 to 1934, scoring 7,037 runs at 44.53 and being made captain in 1932 and 1933. Jack Hobbs said that, after Percy Fender, he was the best captain he had ever played under. However, it is for the immensely controversial 'Bodyline' tour of Australia in 1932/33 – which he led as England captain and advocated the policy of aggressively bowling at batsmen's bodies – that he will always be remembered. Following this tour, Jardine enjoyed a final successful summer in England and led a further tour of India before retiring ahead of a potential controversial home Ashes series in 1934. In retirement Jardine was a successful cricket journalist and served honourably in the Second World War, receiving injuries but successfully escaping from Dunkirk.

18th JUNE 2006

Surrey lost to Gloucestershire by two runs in the South Division of the Cheltenham and Gloucester Trophy at the County Ground in Bristol, despite opener James Benning's unbeaten 189, the third-highest one-day score for the club. Benning's was a rather lonely effort that came up just short despite a 57-run partnership for the final wicket with Neil Saker.

18th JUNE 2012

Young batsman Tom Maynard was tragically killed in the early hours of the morning. After playing in a Twenty20 game against Kent at Beckenham, Maynard was driving in Wimbledon in the early hours of the morning when his car was pulled over by the police. Maynard fled the scene and was electrocuted when attempting to cross the nearby District Line. His loss was deeply felt by all in cricket with Surrey chairman Richard Thompson saying: 'There is a profound sense of loss at the passing of Tom. To lose anybody at such a young age is an utterly senseless tragedy.'

18th JUNE 1925

Cambridge University successfully completed the largest last-innings chase against Surrey with 427/4 to win at The Oval by six wickets. Eddie Dawson, who would go on to play Test cricket for England, scored 125 as the students beat a side containing Jack Hobbs, Andy Ducat, Douglas Jardine and Bill Hitch by six wickets.

19th JUNE 1999

Surrey dismissed Glamorgan for 44 at The Oval in the CGU National League, the lowest one-day score registered against the club. Adam Hollioake had won the toss and batted first, but Surrey only scored 187 from 45 overs. However, with Martin Bicknell's 7-30 – the best one-day figures ever for Surrey – Hollioake's men cut through their opposition to win by 143 runs.

19th JUNE 2002

Alistair Brown continued Surrey's habit of setting one-day scoring records as he blasted 268 from 160 balls against Glamorgan in the Cheltenham & Gloucester Trophy at The Oval. Surrey's final score of 438/5 was, at the time, the highest one-day team score ever made.

DOUGLAS JARDINE, THE ENGLAND CAPTAIN AT THE HEART OF THE BODYLINE CONTROVERSY

20th JUNE 2003

James Anderson took a hat-trick at The Oval during England's one-day international against Pakistan. Anderson ended the Pakistan innings by dismissing Abdul Razzaq, Shoaib Akhtar and Mohammad Sami in consecutive deliveries to keep the tourists to just 180 with England mopping up the runs required from exactly 22 overs.

20th JUNE 2005

Adam Hollioake came out of retirement to play for an International XI against an Asia XI in a Twenty20 match at The Oval, staged to raise funds for the victims of the Indian Ocean tsunami that had struck earlier that year. In front of a sell-out crowd of 23,000, Hollioake took a hat-trick he modestly described as 'the worst you will ever see' as 91* from Australian Greg Blewett saw the International XI win a game that, more importantly, raised £1.1m for charitable causes.

21st JUNE 1909

Surrey played their only first-class game at Park Lane in Reigate, a three-day match against Oxford University. Sadly, it was unhappy trip for a Surrey side captained by John Shuter, who lost heavily, by an innings and 98 runs.

21st JUNE 1937

The great John Edrich was born in Blofield, Norfolk. Edrich began his first-class career for the Combined Services while completing his National Service and played his first game for Surrey at the end of the 1958 season. He continued to play for the club until the end of the 1978 season, making 410 first-class appearances, scoring 29,305 runs and becoming the fourth Surrey player to make 100 first-class centuries. After the retirement of Micky Stewart at the end of 1972, Edrich was appointed captain of the club until 1977, and he retired after the 1978 season. Edrich was also one of England's finest Test players of the 1960s and 1970s, playing 77 times and scoring 5,138 runs at an average of 43.54, becoming – at Headingley in 1965 – just the fourth Englishman to hit a Test match triple century after Andy Sandham, Wally Hammond and Len Hutton. In his retirement, Edrich served as president of Surrey in 2006.

21st JUNE 1962

Micky Stewart made his Test debut against Pakistan at Lord's. Stewart was a far greater player for Surrey than England but played eight Tests between 1962 and 1964. During this time he achieved a very creditable aggregate of 385 runs at an average of 35. However, as with a number of his illustrious colleagues past and in the future, England's loss was to be Surrey's gain.

22nd JUNE 1997

Surrey travelled to Worcester to play an AXA Life League match against Worcestershire. At 59/8, humiliation was on the cards but a partnership of 83 between Saqlain Mushtaq and Martin Bicknell, whose unbeaten 57 was Surrey's highest ever one-day score from number nine, saw them to 149 all out, a total easily reached by Worcestershire who won by seven wickets.

23rd JUNE 1971

Christopher Martin-Jenkins, later better known as a journalist and broadcaster, played his one and only game of 'professional' cricket when he represented the Surrey second XI at The Oval against Warwickshire. Records of the three-day match are scarce but Surrey drew the game and CMJ was in good company with New Zealand international and future Surrey captain Geoff Howarth and West Indian legend Alvin Kallicharran also playing.

23rd JUNE 2005

Fast bowler Tim Murtagh recorded Surrey's best Twenty20 bowling figures with 6-24 against Middlesex at Lord's in a derby win by 23 runs.

23rd JUNE 2006

Martin Bicknell played his final first-class game, against Glamorgan in Swansea. Having originally intended to retire at the end of the season, a series of niggling injuries caused the great seamer to hang up his boots three months early.

23rd JUNE 2010

Batsman Jason Roy became the first Surrey player to hit a century in Twenty20 cricket, smashing a brilliant 101 from 57 balls against Kent in Beckenham as his side romped to victory by 38 runs.

24th JUNE 1926

Jack Hobbs and Andy Sandham batted all day against Oxford University at The Oval as they built their record partnership of 428 for the first wicket. The two started at the end of the first day, batted through the second and were split on the third morning, just 20 runs short of the all-time club record – held by Bobby Abel and Tom Hayward – when Sandham fell for 183. The game ended in a draw.

24th JUNE 1967

Darren Bicknell was born in Guildford, 18 months before his younger brother Martin. Darren made his Surrey debut in 1987 and was a stalwart of the side throughout the 1990s, playing 195 times and scoring 12,464 runs at an average of 40.20. He left at the end of the 1999 season and spent seven years at Nottinghamshire before retiring in 2006.

24th JUNE 2007

Surrey re-signed Indian spinner Harbhajan Singh, who had already enjoyed a spell at the club in 2005. The return would prove to a successful one with Harbhajan taking 37 wickets at 18.54 and Surrey finishing fourth in the County Championship Division One.

25th JUNE 1846

Surrey played their first 'County Match' against Kent at The Oval. Kent batted first and the opening delivery at The Oval was by fast bowler Daniel Day to Kent batsman Alfred Mynn. Surrey eventually won the game by ten wickets, chasing down four to win in the final innings.

25th JUNE 1986

The great Laurie Fishlock sadly died in hospital in Sutton following an operation. He was 79.

25th JUNE 2009

Surrey slipped to their biggest Twenty20 defeat as a century from Essex opener Alastair Cook condemned a side led by Usman Afzaal to an 84-run defeat at The Oval. The game was also notable for Chris Schofield conceding a club record in Twenty20 cricket of 54 runs from his four overs.

25th JUNE 2010

Exactly one year on from that heavy defeat to Essex, Surrey became the away side as they travelled to Chelmsford to face the same opposition. Despite 89 from Steven Davies and a very good team total of 187/6, Scott Styris hit a brutal 106* from 50 balls – the highest individual Twenty20 score made against Surrey – to give Essex a six-wicket victory off the penultimate ball of the match.

26th JUNE 1888

Walter Read became the first man to hit a triple century for Surrey when he scored 338 against Oxford University at The Oval. Read was

235* overnight and continued batting on the second day, reaching the landmark after 390 minutes and having hit 46 boundaries. Sadly, his feat did not achieve victory with poor weather meaning the game was called a draw on the final day.

26th JUNE 1919

Andy Ducat hit 306* in a day for Surrey against Oxford University at The Oval. Ducat came to the crease at the fall of the first wicket and batted all day, eventually reaching his landmark score – a career best – after 280 minutes. He hit 47 fours and three sixes, helping Surrey to 523 all out and victory by an innings and 47 runs.

26th JUNE 1983

Surrey played their only game at the Hurst Park Club Ground in East Molesey, a John Player League match against Northamptonshire. Surrey's innings – led by Alan Butcher and Monte Lynch – totalled 232/6 but was comfortably bettered by their visitors' 234/5 as Northants took a five-wicket win.

26th JUNE 1992

Mark Butcher made his first-class debut in a County Championship match against Gloucestershire in Bristol. When the hosts batted first, Butcher actually opened the bowling alongside Tony Murphy, putting down ten overs for just 20 runs. Although he did not bat in the first innings, Butcher was at the crease as Surrey successfully chased down 232/6 to win on the final day.

27th JUNE 1984

Surrey played their only game at the Recreation Ground in Banstead, a three-day match against Cambridge University. The draw is notable for being the first-class debuts of Keith Medlycott and Nick Falkner, who both marked the occasion with centuries.

27th JUNE 2006

Surrey recorded their highest Twenty20 score during a London derby at Lord's against Middlesex. Big-hitting openers James Benning and Alistair Brown got Surrey off to a flyer with a club record partnership of 148 before skipper Rikki Clarke helped the final total to 218/7. After being 5/3 and then 13/4, Middlesex never looked like getting close and ended on 178/7 – a 40-run win for Surrey.

28th JUNE 2006

Surrey recorded their biggest Twenty20 win, against Kent at The Oval. Batting first, 88 from James Benning and 58 from Mark Ramprakash saw the then-Brown Caps to 198/6. In reply, spin twins Ian Salisbury and Nayan Doshi strangled the Kent response as they quickly slipped to 91 all out, giving Surrey a huge win by 107 runs.

28th JUNE 2011

Jade Dernbach made his one-day international debut at The Oval, just days after having made his Twenty20 international debut at Bristol. In a rain-affected first match in the series, England scored 229/8 and Dernbach – coming on first change – removed Thilina Kandamby and Angelo Matthews to record good figures of 2-25.

29th JUNE 2007

Surrey travelled to Hove to play the Sussex Sharks and posted a defendable target of 168/6. Four wickets from Chris Schofield then saw the Sharks blown away for just 68, the lowest Twenty20 total against Surrey.

30th JUNE 1913

Andy Sandham and Henry Harrison added 298 for the sixth wicket during a County Championship game against Sussex at The Oval. Their partnership is still a club record today and Surrey won the match by an innings and 158 runs.

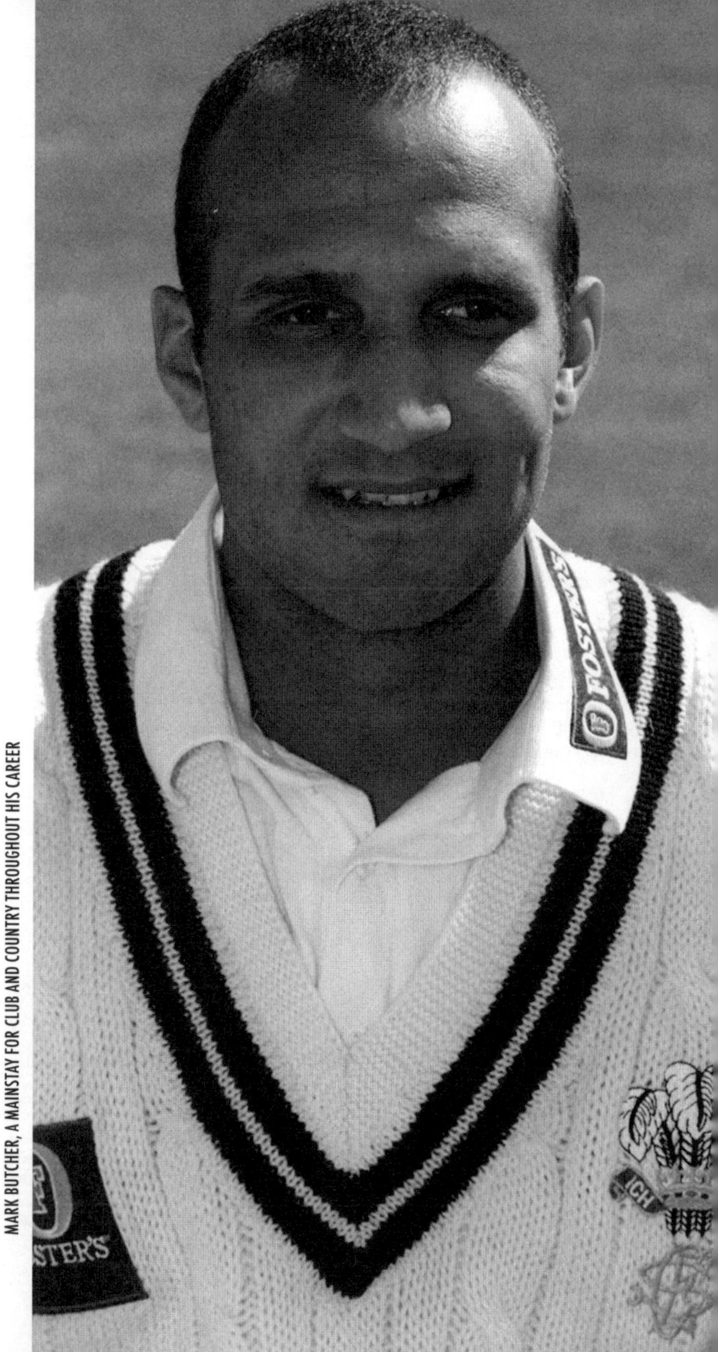

MARK BUTCHER, A MAINSTAY FOR CLUB AND COUNTRY THROUGHOUT HIS CAREER

SURREY CCC
On This Day

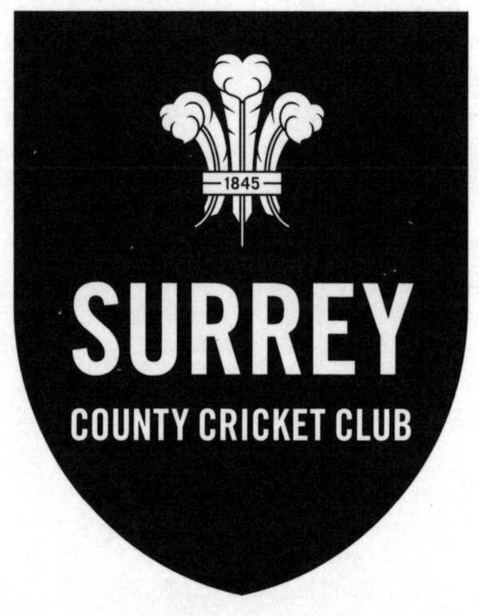

JULY

1st JULY 1995

Bruce Mitchell died aged 86 in Abbotsford, Johannesburg. Mitchell's claim to fame at The Oval is as the ground's leading Test run scorer from a nation other than England or Australia, who it could be argued have an advantage as the two countries had played 11 Tests there before any other country visited for the first time in 1907. South African Mitchell scored 120 and 189* in the 1947 Oval Test, batting for more than 13 hours.

2nd JULY 2004

During a Twenty20 group match at Hove, Sussex seamer James Kirtley was taken for 63 runs from his four overs – the most a bowler has conceded against Surrey in the format. Predictably, much of the damage was done by Alistair Brown, who hit 45 from 24 balls as Surrey reached 221/8. In reply, Sussex managed 121 as Adam Hollioake took 4-14 from three overs and Brown bowled the only two deliveries of his Twenty20 career.

3rd JULY 2002

Surrey began an extraordinary County Championship Division One match at Taunton against Somerset. By the end of the first day, Surrey had recovered from 0/1 and 32/2 to post 448/5, with Mark Ramprakash 199*. The second day saw Ramprakash reach his double century and Rikki Clarke amass 153* as Surrey declared on 608/6. In response, Somerset hit 554 all out in their first innings. Then 151 from Jonathan Batty lifted Surrey to 324/5 declared in their second innings, leaving Somerset an unlikely 378 to win on the final afternoon. Their eventual 329/7 meant the game – which had seen a club record tally of 1,815 runs scored across the four days – was drawn.

3rd JULY 1999

Alex Tudor became a national hero when his 99*, scored from number three as a night-watchman, led England to victory over New Zealand at Edgbaston. Batting at the end with Graham Thorpe, Tudor came agonisingly close to a maiden Test hundred but was named Man of the Match. His performance was so impressive that Scyld Berry speculated in the *Daily Telegraph* that the game might mark the start of a 'Tudor age' for English cricket.

4th JULY 1911

It is not often that a number 11 batsman is your side's top scorer but in Surrey's match with Warwickshire at Edgbaston in 1911 that was exactly the case. Chasing down 501, Surrey had reached 182/9 and were in dire trouble. However, Bill Hitch – more commonly known as a demon fast bowler – combined with wicketkeeper Bert Strudwick to deliver a scintillating 130-run partnership for the last wicket. Hitch's total of 82 remains the largest score ever made by a Surrey number 11.

4th JULY 1918

A great day for Surrey County Cricket Club, though nobody knew at the time, as Eric Arthur Bedser (first) and Alec Victor Bedser (second) were born in Reading. The twins moved to Woking aged six months and never left. They excelled as young cricketers and – after nearly becoming solicitors – were spotted by Surrey coach Alan Peach and recommended to Surrey officials. The epitome of identical twins, the Bedser brothers were never separated and made their first-class debuts in the same match, against Oxford University at The Oval in June 1939. They each only played one more game, against Cambridge University, before going to war where they successfully escaped from Dunkirk and served in North Africa, Italy and Austria. They were demobilised in May 1946 and immediately became mainstays of the Surrey side. Their only difference was in international recognition, with Alec becoming one of England's finest ever bowlers while Eric, despite his consistently good performances for Surrey, was never given a chance in the Test arena.

4th JULY 1921

In the middle of his only Test, against Australia at Headingley, Andy Ducat walked out to bat on the third morning hoping to add to his overnight score of 3*. He had yet to score when he faced up to Australian Ted McDonald and attempted to steer a delivery through the covers. Sadly while doing so he broke the shoulder of his bat and only succeeded in gently lobbing the ball to slip. To make matters worse, the shard of wood that had flown off his bat then somehow managed to remove the bails, effectively dismissing him twice. Ducat only scored two in the second innings and never played Test cricket again.

5th JULY 1929

Graham Anthony Richard 'Tony' Lock was born in Limpsfield. Lock made his first-class debut against Kent in 1946 but despite a handful of appearances, did not become a regular until 1949 when he formed his now legendary partnership with Jim Laker. Lock played 385 times for Surrey and took 1,713 wickets – second on the all-time list and just 62 behind Tom Richardson – at an average of 17.41. He also played 49 Tests, taking a further 174 wickets at 25.58.

6th JULY 1868

Surrey wicketkeeper Ted Pooley set a record that has now stood for 144 years when he claimed 12 victims in the same match against Sussex at The Oval. The game, which Surrey won by seven wickets, saw Pooley make five catches and a stumping in the first innings and three catches and three stumpings in the second. Pooley was the first and is still one of only six men to ever achieve the feat.

6th JULY 1890

Andrew Sandham was born in Streatham. Sandham is the third-leading all-time run scorer for the club, one of only five Surrey players to hit more than 100 first-class centuries and the first man to ever hit a Test triple century. He served the club throughout his life, first as a batsman, then as a coach and finally as a scorer. He was remembered in his *Wisden* obituary as: 'A quiet man with a great sense of humour, who set himself and expected of others a high standard of behaviour, he was much respected.'

6th JULY 1921

Tom Rushby took the first nine wickets of his ten-wicket haul for Surrey against Somerset at the County Ground in Taunton. Somerset ended the day on 89/9, with right-arm seamer Rushby having bowled unchanged to take all nine. The following morning Rushby had Stanley Amor caught by Andy Sandham for 19 to complete his full house as Surrey won by 229 runs. His final figures of 10-43 are still the cheapest of all five Surrey bowlers to have taken all ten.

7th JULY 2001

Surrey needed a massive 535 to beat Leicestershire at Grace Road and when they started the final day on 281/6 against an attack including Devon Malcolm, Jimmy Ormond and Phil DeFreitas they were certainly second favourites. However, a brilliant rearguard action led by Alex Tudor and Martin Bicknell and completed when number 11 Ian Salisbury faced 127 balls for his 30* saw Surrey bat through the day to end unbowed on 478/9, the club's highest ever score in a fourth innings.

8th JULY 1965

England played New Zealand in the third Test at Headingley and M.J.K. Smith won the toss and batted first. John Edrich opened the batting and saw his partner, Warwickshire's Bob Barber, dismissed early by Bruce Taylor. That was the last success New Zealand saw all day though as Edrich and his Surrey and England team-mate Ken Barrington ruled the roost. The pair put on 369 for the second wicket, the highest for any wicket at a Headingley Test. At 194* overnight, Edrich went on to a brilliant career best of 310* as England posted 546/4 and won by an innings and 187 runs.

8th JULY 2005

Surrey achieved the amazing feat of playing an innings where seven individual batsmen hit fifties – only the second time in club history it has been achieved. The innings – of 603 all out against Gloucestershire in Bristol – featured half-centuries from openers Scott Newman and Richard Clinton, number three Graham Thorpe, number five Jonathan Batty, number seven Azhar Mahmood, number eight Martin Bicknell and number nine Harbhajan Singh. The game ended in a draw but Surrey certainly claimed all five batting bonus points.

8th JULY 2008

This was the day when the unthinkable became possible and Middlesex played a home fixture at The Oval. The then-Crusaders had made it into the knockout stages at the expense of Surrey, who finished bottom of the South Group, but could not play their home quarter-final at Lord's because of the ongoing Test there. They 'borrowed' The Oval and made good use of it as they beat Lancashire by 12 runs.

9th JULY 1908

George Edwards was born in Highams Park, North London. A highly successful aircraft designer, Edwards led the team who designed the Valiant strategic bomber and Valetta military transport plane before becoming executive director of the new British Aircraft Corporation (BAC), where he led the British part of the team responsible for the design of Concorde. He retired from BAC, as chairman, in 1975 and in 1979 was appointed Surrey president. He died in 2003, nine years before a fast bowling namesake of his joined the Surrey professional staff. Edwards had been knighted in 1957 and was later made a member of the Order of Merit and awarded the Royal Medal.

9th JULY 2002

Essex's Ronnie Irani took 5-26 in a one-day international against India at The Oval. The figures remain the best by an Englishman in an ODI at the ground.

10th JULY 1937

The Oval staged its first international women's match when England played Australia in the third Test of a series that was eventually drawn

1-1. The day's play saw Australia bat first and end on 201/8 with Joan Davis taking five wickets.

10th JULY 1956

Tony Lock recorded career best figures of 10-54 as, at The Rectory Field in Blackheath, he bowled out the entire Kent side to give Surrey victory by an innings and 173 runs. Lock's overall match figures were 16-83, still the best ever match return by a Surrey bowler.

10th JULY 2006

The Oval hosted its second all-star charity match in two years when an International XI took on Pakistan in a Twenty20 fixture to raise money for the survivors of an earthquake in Pakistan. Sadly, rain and gloom reduced the spectacle to just ten overs a side but fans still got to watch Sachin Tendulkar, Brian Lara and Mahendra Singh Dhoni score 123/1 in their ten overs before an even more brutal barrage from Shahid Afridi settled the game in favour of the Pakistanis.

11th JULY 1890

Arthur Tedder was born at the Glenguin Distillery, north of Glasgow. After joining the Army in 1913 he rose rapidly through the ranks during the First World War, joining the Royal Flying Corps and ending the war as a lieutenant colonel. During the Second World War, Tedder served in North Africa – once again ascending through the ranks quickly – and served as deputy to General Dwight D. Eisenhower when he was appointed as Deputy Supreme Commander of the Allied Expeditionary Force, signing for Eisenhower in May 1945 when the unconditional surrender of all Germans was announced. At the end of the war he was promoted to Marshal of the Royal Air Force. He held a number of senior peacetime jobs before retiring in 1951. In retirement, as well as serving as vice-chairman of the BBC and chairman of the Standard Motor Company, he was president of Surrey CCC from 1953 to 1958, having become the first Baron Tedder in 1946.

11th JULY 1953

Peter Loader took then career-best figures of 9-28 against Kent at Blackheath. His brilliant burst – spoilt only by the run out of number ten batsman Doug Wright – skittled Kent for just 63, allowing Surrey opener David Fletcher to end the day on 105*. Despite this, the game was drawn after Kent managed 323 in their second innings.

BRIAN LARA AND SACHIN TENDULKAR AT A 2006 T20 MATCH TO RAISE FUNDS FOR THE SURVIVORS OF AN EARTHQUAKE IN PAKISTAN

12th JULY 1970

Surrey played their first game at the British Aerospace Company Ground in Byfleet – a John Player League match against Warwickshire, which they lost by five wickets after posting 196/7 from their 40 overs. Surrey would go on to play a one-day match there for each of the next nine years. Their record there is five wins, four defeats and a tie with Worcestershire in 1973.

12th JULY 1992

Martin Bicknell took a hat-trick during Surrey's Sunday League victory over Derbyshire at The Oval. Bicknell had Derbyshire skipper John Morris caught behind by Alec Stewart, then West Indian Ian Bishop caught by James Boiling and finally wicketkeeper Karl Krikken caught by Mark Feltham. Surrey eventually won by three wickets, Stewart top scoring with 86.

12th JULY 1997

Surrey won the Benson & Hedges Cup after beating Kent by eight wickets in a one-sided final at Lord's. Kent won the toss and batted first, scoring 212/9 from their 50 overs with Chris Lewis taking 3-39. Surrey lost Alistair Brown for just two but a 159-run partnership between Alec Stewart (75*) and Ben Hollioake (98) saw them home with five overs in reserve.

13th JULY 1938

Surrey started their first game at the Guildford Festival, winning the toss and batting against Hampshire. The first ever ball at Woodbridge Road was bowled by right-arm quick Lofty Herman to Laurie Fishlock. It was a successful first day for Monty Garland-Wells's side, who ended 371/6 with Edward Whitfield 98*. He would go on to to complete his ton with Surrey comfortably winning by an innings and 71 runs.

13th JULY 2012

Kevin Pietersen played one of the most memorable innings ever seen in Guildford, a sensational 234* from 190 balls. On a balmy Friday afternoon, Pietersen dispatched the Lancashire bowling to all corners of the ground – including at least one six which cleared the large tree that guards the leg-side boundary from the Pavilion End. Sadly a full day of rain prevented Pietersen from starting up again the following morning and the match was drawn.

14th JULY 1902

Surrey started a County Championship match against Sussex at Hastings but lost the toss and had a poor day with Sussex ending on 419/6. However, the pain was not over and the following day the great Ranjitsinhji transformed his overnight 54* to 234*, propelling his side to 705/8 declared, the second-highest total ever conceded by Surrey.

14th JULY 1961

Needing 203 to beat Leicestershire at The Oval, Surrey were dramatically bowled out for 201. On 164/4, they seemed to be cruising but a dramatic late collapse saw the club lose a first-class match by one run for what is still the only time in its history.

15th JULY 2001

Surrey won the Benson & Hedges Cup for the second time in four years, beating Gloucestershire at Lord's by 47 runs. Skipper Adam Hollioake won the toss and batted first, with his brother Ben (73) and Ian Ward (54) confidently leading the way to 244 all out. Jack Russell – opening for Gloucestershire – always looked dangerous but when he was caught behind by Alec Stewart off Alex Tudor, Surrey quickly closed the door with Saqlain Mushtaq and Ed Giddins taking three wickets each as Gloucestershire fell to 197 all out. Ben Hollioake was named Man of the Match.

15th JULY 2005

Surrey played Hampshire at The Oval in the quarter-final of the Cheltenham and Gloucester Trophy. Mark Ramprakash opted to bat first and would have been delighted to see his side rack up a brilliant 358/6 – largely thanks to a career-best 158* from Jonathan Batty. However Hampshire, emboldened by their young Australian all-rounder Shane Watson's 132 from 105 balls, set about the total aggressively and surpassed it with more than two overs remaining to advance to the semi-finals.

16th JULY 1953

Surrey declared their first innings at The Oval closed overnight on 371/6 and then took 12 wickets in the day against Worcestershire in the County Championship. Eight of these fell to the brilliant Peter Loader, who returned figures of 8-21 as the opposition went down for just 82 then Stuart Surridge and Eric Bedser made early inroads into the second innings as they closed on 34/2.

16th JULY 1954

Day three of the County Championship game between Surrey and Gloucestershire at The Oval started with a draw looking by far the most likely result. Surrey were just 10/1 and had a lead of only 31. This was quickly added to with David Fletcher hitting 89 and Ken Barrington 68 to allow Stuart Surridge to declare on 202/7 and set Gloucestershire 223 to win. The draw was still odds on but Jim Laker was able to draw veracious turn from the last-day pitch and took 6-20 on the final afternoon as Surrey clinched a superb victory by 145 runs.

17th JULY 1952

Tony Lock made his Test debut against India in the third Test at Old Trafford. His first two days were very relaxed, as England batted through showers for the first two and a half days to score 347/9 declared. He then did not bowl in the first innings as Fred Trueman's 8-31 dismissed India for just 58. The young left-arm spinner got his chance in the second innings though, contributing 4-36 as India managed 82, losing by an innings and 207 runs.

17th JULY 1998

One of the more satisfying days for Surrey fans, as the club recorded their biggest first-class victory over bitter rivals Middlesex at Guildford. Starting the final day on 335/8 in their second innings, 61 from Ian Salisbury and 41 from Alex Tudor lifted them to 420 all out, setting Middlesex a giant 456 to win. Salisbury then impressed with the ball, taking 4-43 as Middlesex fell away for just 175, falling to defeat by 280 runs.

18th JULY 1919

Middlesex, having been 503/7 overnight, continued batting in their County Championship match at The Oval to reach 568/9 declared with centuries from Harry Lee, Jack Hearne and Leslie Kidd. The score remains the largest they have ever achieved against Surrey.

18th JULY 2010

Surrey finished their Twenty20 campaign for the year against Gloucestershire at Bristol. The game was won by six wickets thanks to 73 from just 30 balls from Steven Davies and an amazing three-ball innings from Gary Wilson, consisting of just a six and two fours. As the game ended, Rory Hamilton-Brown – with 397 runs – and Chris Tremlett – with 24 wickets – both walked off the pitch with new season aggregate records for Surrey.

19th JULY 1849

Surrey sent a side to the county of Sussex for the first time, starting a game at Petworth Park New Ground. The trip was not a ringing success for the club, with the side losing by an innings and 49 runs.

19th JULY 1939

Great batsman Tom Hayward sadly passed away in Cambridge aged 68. Hayward started his Surrey career in 1893 and played until August 1914. During this time he amassed an astonishing 36,171 runs, including 88 hundreds. In his book, *The History of Surrey County Cricket Club*, David Lemmon said of Hayward: 'He was the senior professional in all aspects, setting down standards of behaviour which others violated at their peril. He led by bearing and by example.'

19th JULY 2003

Surrey won the inaugural Twenty20 Cup on the first Finals Day, held at Trent Bridge in Nottingham. Having beaten Gloucestershire earlier that day in the semi-final, Surrey were exceptional against Warwickshire. First they bowled out the opposition for just 115 – with Jimmy Ormond taking 4-11 – then Ian Ward and Alistair Brown both got half-centuries as Surrey won by nine wickets with more than eight overs remaining. The game might not have had the dramatic finish many neutrals had hoped for but it was a fitting end to a tournament Surrey had dominated from start to finish.

20th JULY 1908

Surrey won the toss and batted first against Hampshire at the United Services Ground in Portsmouth. They batted excellently all day, ending on 485/7 and – for one of only two occasions in club history – had seven individual batsmen post half-centuries. On this occasion the runs were scored by Tom Hayward, Jack Hobbs, Ernie Hayes, Alan Marshal, Jack Crawford, Frederick Holland and William Spring.

20th JULY 1974

Surrey won their first limited overs trophy, defeating Leicestershire by 27 runs at Lord's. Batting first, Surrey managed just 170 all out but bowled superbly to dismiss the opposition for just 143 with three wickets for both Geoff Arnold and Pat Pocock.

20th JULY 1997

Alistair Brown became the fifth batsman in history to a one-day double century as he hit 203 in Surrey's AXA Life League victory over Hampshire at Guildford. It was the first double century ever in a 40-over match.

21st JULY 1851

Surrey played their first game against Yorkshire at Hyde Park, Sheffield, winning a two-day encounter by 72 runs.

21st JULY 2000

Martin Bicknell completed incredible match figures of 16-119 in Surrey's ten-wicket win over Leicestershire at Woodbridge Road, Guildford. Bicknell took 7-72 in the first innings, returning to take 9-47 in the second, only being denied all ten when Carl Greenidge trapped Ben Smith lbw. Of all of the great bowlers to have represented Surrey throughout the years, Bicknell, alongside Tony Lock, remains one of only two to have taken 16 wickets in a single game.

21st JULY 2006

Rikki Clarke started his career-best innings of 214 during Surrey's County Championship match with Somerset at Guildford. The knock helped Surrey achieve the unlikely feat of overhauling Somerset's 688/8 and is the highest ever scored for the club from number six.

22nd JULY 1979

Surrey played their tenth and final game at the British Aerospace Company Ground in Byfleet, a three-wicket win over Warwickshire. The – very good – reason games had to cease on the ground was because it was situated right in the middle of the planned route of the new circular motorway the M25.

22nd JULY 1993

Martin Bicknell made his England Test debut at Headingley, taking 1-155 from 50 overs in a hefty defeat to Australia, who scored 653/4 in the first innings. Bicknell was kept on for the next Test – another chastening defeat – but then had to wait another decade to represent his country once again.

22nd JULY 2002

Surrey completed their highest successful fourth-innings chase when they scored 410/8 against Kent at Canterbury, Ian Ward starring with 168*. Surrey had seemed out of it at 208/7 but 60 from Saqlain Mushtaq and

43* from Jimmy Ormond allowed the battling Ward to take it home in glorious fashion.

23rd JULY 1846

Surrey played their first away game when they made the trip to Preston Hall Ground in Aylesford to play Kent. Having beaten them at The Oval the previous month, Surrey would have been keen for a repeat performance but were unable to force the victory with Kent hanging on at 29/7 when rain arrived at 3pm on the final day and saved them from the twin threats of Surrey bowlers Daniel Day and George Brockwell.

23rd JULY 1859

Surrey crashed to their heaviest runs defeat in a match against England at The Oval. Surrey only conceded a 41-run deficit on the first innings, then England captain Edward Walker hit 108 in the second innings, leading his side to 390 all out. In reply Surrey totally folded as they were dismissed for just 39 – John Jackson taking 6-21 – as England won by 392 runs.

23rd JULY 1915

All-rounder Alan Marshal died in Imtarfa Military Hospital, Malta. Marshal was born in Queensland in 1883 but moved to London in 1905. He qualified to play for Surrey in 1907 and played 98 times for the club, scoring 4,195 runs and taking 101 wickets. His final match for Surrey was in May 1910, against Warwickshire at Edgbaston. In the First World War, Marshal, among the Australian troops sent to Gallipoli, caught enteric fever and was evacuated to Malta, where he died.

23rd JULY 1942

Andy Ducat, a great batsman for Surrey who also played international football for England, died at the crease at Lord's. After his retirement, Ducat, according to *Wisden*, was 'well-set-up, vigorous, healthy-looking and careful-living'. Aged 53, the then Private Ducat turned out for the Surrey Home Guard against the Sussex Home Guard at Lord's. Ducat was 17* at lunch and, after the break, took his score on to 29 from where his team-mate that day, Bob Attwell, can pick up the story. 'Andy hit the ball past me to mid-on,' he said, 'and I was returning to the crease after backing-up and I heard a gasp ... I turned round and saw Andy on his back.'

23rd JULY 1949

Freddie Brown led England for the first time, against New Zealand at Old Trafford. The game, as with all four Tests that summer, was drawn. Brown, who had played for Surrey until the outbreak of the Second World

War, ended up captaining his country a further 14 times. While at war, Brown was awarded the MBE for his work in the evacuation of Crete, an operation run by future Surrey president Air Marshal Arthur Tedder.

23rd JULY 1953

Graham Alan Gooch was born in Whipps Cross, Leytonstone, Essex. Although often an adversarial figure for Surrey, averaging exactly 50 against the club in 46 innings, Gooch is the only man other than Sir Len Hutton to score more than 1,000 Test runs at The Oval, averaging an impressive 52.23 in 22 innings.

24th JULY 2003

Jimmy Ormond completed a first-class hat-trick during Surrey's drawn match with Middlesex at Guildford. With Surrey defending a first-innings total of 411, Ormond removed Ben Hutton, Ed Joyce and Paul Weekes in successive deliveries.

24th JULY 2006

Surrey scored their highest total in Twenty20 cricket during a match away against Gloucestershire at Bristol. Mark Ramprakash's 85 and 79* from Rikki Clarke helped Surrey notch 224/5 which they easily defended with off-spinner Nayan Doshi taking 4-25.

25th JULY 1957

Peter Loader completed a Test hat-trick against the West Indies during the fourth Test at Headingley. Loader took the wickets of John Goddard, Sonny Ramadhin and Roy Gilchrist as he secured excellent figures of 6-36. Despite only making 279, England won the game by an innings and five runs.

25th JULY 2002

Alec Stewart became England's most capped Test cricketer of all time when he was selected to play in a 170-run victory over India at Lord's. It was his 119th cap and saw him overtake the previous record holder Graham Gooch.

26th JULY 1919

Pre-war great Ernie Hayes played his final match for Surrey, against Kent at Blackheath. Hayes had made his Surrey debut in 1896 and played regularly until 1914 when he left for the First World War, in which he served with the Sportsman's Battalion. Sadly for Hayes his final game for the club saw him score just one and seven.

26th JULY 2002

Surrey were engaged in a tough County Championship match with Yorkshire at Guildford and – after securing a good first-innings lead – were having trouble dismissing their opponents for a second time. Wicketkeeper Richard Blakey was anchoring the innings and dispatched a sweep directly into the press tent. Sadly for Blakey this woke Bumper, a slumbering Labrador belonging to *Times* journalist Geoff Dean. Following his natural instinct, Bumper took the ball in his mouth and, when it was eventually returned to boundary fielder Rikki Clarke, there were added tooth marks and saliva. Umpire Nigel Llong refused to allow Surrey to change the ball for another of similar age, effectively forcing Adam Hollioake to take the recently available new ball and – through no fault of his own – abandon his spin strategy. The enforced change worked, with the returning Jimmy Ormond, Ed Giddins and Clarke wrapping up the Yorkshire innings, leaving Surrey just 237 to win – a target that was reached thanks to a superb 124* from Ian Ward and 59 from night-watchman Ian Salisbury.

27th JULY 1880

Surrey were dismissed for just 16 in a game against Nottinghamshire at The Oval. Having conceded 266 in the first innings, a side skippered by Bunny Lucas fell victim to Fred Morley and Alfred Shaw, who bowled all of the 39.2 overs that were required.

28th JULY 1936

The great Sir Garfield St Auburn Sobers was born in St Michael, Barbados. As with many West Indian cricketers, Sobers enjoyed playing at The Oval. His record at the ground from 12 first-class matches is 1,034 runs including two centuries and a best of 160 as well as 22 wickets.

29th JULY 1828

Frederick Miller, the captain of Surrey from 1851 to 1857 and president of the club from 1867 to 1878, was born in Clapham. Miller played 80 times for Surrey, taking 131 wickets at 20.86 and scoring 1,540 runs at 13.05. He has a historical reputation as a fine captain with Nottinghamshire player Jem Grundy claiming his captaincy was worth 50 runs in the field.

29th JULY 1931

New Zealand started a Test at The Oval for the first time, an eventual loss by an innings and 26 runs to an England side captained by Surrey's Douglas Jardine and also featuring his club-mate Freddie Brown. The victory gave England a 1-0 series win in a three-game series.

29th JULY 2004

Adam Hollioake started his final game of first-class cricket, a four-wicket defeat to Northamptonshire at the County Ground, Northampton. Under the captaincy of Jonathan Batty, Hollioake hit 76 in the first innings as Surrey scored 402. After recording a 70-run lead, Surrey were then bowled out for just 147 in the second innings – Hollioake scoring one – allowing Northamptonshire to easily reach their target of 218.

30th JULY 1868

Fast bowler James Street took the first hat-trick in Surrey colours. Sadly his exact victims were not recorded – but it was 17 years before another was taken, by medium-pacer William Roller.

30th JULY 1968

Ken Barrington played his last day of Test cricket, a drawn fourth Test against Australia at Headingley. Appropriately for the stoic middle-order star he walked off, alongside debutant Keith Fletcher, unbeaten on 46.

30th JULY 1978

In a rain-affected John Player League match at New Road, Worcester Surrey were bowled out for just 64, a total that still stands as the club's lowest in their history in that format. The primary element of destruction was Worcestershire bowler Paul Pridgeon who took 6-26.

30th JULY 1982

James Michael Anderson was born in Burnley. Anderson is the leading one-day international wicket-taker in the history of The Oval, taking 25 scalps in his 12 matches at just 19.64 each.

30th JULY 2005

The Oval hosted Twenty20 Finals Day for the only time. Surrey had made it to the semi-finals for the third consecutive year but sadly, there was to be no glorious home victory as, in the first semi, Surrey conceded a club record 214/4 to a strong Lancashire side including Andrew Flintoff and Andrew Symonds. The chase of 195/7 was very creditable but sadly 22 runs short of victory. Somerset – for whom future Surrey skipper Graeme Smith scored 64 from 47 balls – won the final by seven wickets. Elsewhere, Carmen the Bear from Warwickshire was the winner of the ever popular Mascot Derby and a young pop band called Girls Aloud performed to a small crowd in a large rain storm during the gap between the semi-final and final.

31st JULY 1956

Jim Laker completed one of the finest achievements in the history of cricket when he finished the fourth Test against Australia at Old Trafford with match figures of 19-90. The only wicket not taken by Laker was the third to fall in the tourists' first innings, Jim Burke, who was caught by Colin Cowdrey off the bowling of Laker's ubiquitous sidekick Tony Lock. His figures of 10-53 in the second innings remain the best ever in Test cricket and, 57 years later, he is still the only man in the history of first-class cricket to take 19 wickets in a match. What is less reported is how Laker was almost denied his achievement by the notorious Manchester weather – which wiped out all but a tiny amount of play on days three and four. Fortunately for Laker – and England – conditions improved on the final day and he took the final wicket with just over an hour to spare. There was controversy throughout the match, with some of the tourists alleging pitch doctoring in England's favour but, as Australian captain Ian Johnson said: 'When the controversy and side issues of the match are forgotten, Laker's wonderful bowling will remain.'

SURREY CCC
On This Day

AUGUST

1st AUGUST 1866

Surrey fell to their largest ever innings defeat – by an innings and 296 runs – in a match against England at The Oval. After conceding 521 all out in the first innings – with the great W.G. Grace accounting for 224 of them – Edward Dowson's side were always chasing the game. This was made worse when they were dismissed for just 99 in the first innings and completed when – although improved – the second innings could only muster 126 all out.

1st AUGUST 1871

W.G. returned to The Oval to play for the South against the North and was dismissed for a duck in the first innings. However, he was clearly motivated by his uncharacteristic failure and batted throughout the afternoon on day two, reaching 142* overnight. The final day of the match saw Grace go on to record his biggest ever score at The Oval, eventually being dismissed for 268.

1st AUGUST 1887

Club records show that 51,607 people paid for admission to The Oval to watch a closely contested county match between Surrey and Nottinghamshire. In a touch-and-go game, Surrey fought back from a first-innings deficit and chased just over 200 to win – a very tough ask at the time. Captain and opening batsman John Shuter hit 58, with support from Maurice Read and George Lohmann, as they were cheered all the way to a four-wicket victory.

1st AUGUST 1969

Graham Paul Thorpe was born in Farnham. Thorpe came through the Surrey system and made his debut against Leicestershire at The Oval in 1988, batting at number eight and getting through 14 overs in the first innings. He established himself in the Surrey side in 1989 and made his Test debut at Trent Bridge in 1993, scoring an unbeaten 114 in the second innings. The gritty left-hander went on to play 189 times for Surrey, scoring 30 centuries and averaging 44.97. For England, he became one of only two Surrey players to reach the landmark of 100 Tests, scoring 16 hundreds and averaging 44.66.

2nd AUGUST 1992

Adam Hollioake played his first game for Surrey, a Sunday League match at the beautiful Racecourse Ground in Durham. Hollioake hit 22 in Surrey's superb 330/6 – still a one-day record at the ground – and took the wicket of Durham's Ian Smith as Surrey wrapped up a 100-run victory.

2nd AUGUST 2008

Mark Ramprakash recorded his 100th first-class hundred, against Yorkshire at Headingley. Having scored his previous ton against Sussex at Hove in May, the nation's cricket fans were in a state of heightened excitement to see Ramprakash complete the rare feat. However, an uncharacteristic period of poor form left them on edge until early August when the great man forced a cut off young spinner David Wainwright to bring up three figures.

3rd AUGUST 1969

Surrey played their first match at St John's School in Leatherhead, a Player's County League match against Northamptonshire. After bowling the opposition out for just 99 – with Roger Knight taking 4-19 – captain John Edrich top scored with 31 as Surrey won by four wickets.

4th AUGUST 2006

Mark Ramprakash walked out to bat against Northamptonshire on 174* with Surrey in a very strong position on 417/2. With Mark Butcher alongside him, Ramprakash smoothly moved through the gears to become the sixth man to hit a triple century for Surrey – and the first for the club since Jack Hobbs in 1926. He was on 301* when the innings was declared and Surrey went on to win by seven wickets.

4th AUGUST 2010

Surrey hit a then-world record total of 386/3 in their Clydesdale Bank 40 match against Glamorgan. Captain Rory Hamilton-Brown hit 115 from 69 balls with support from Steven Davies (88), Mark Ramprakash (85*) and Matthew Spriegel (56*). Amazingly, the total broke the world record despite the innings being cut short by two overs due to rain. Glamorgan's 187/5 from 20 overs was not quite enough and Surrey won by 39 runs under the Duckworth-Lewis method.

5th AUGUST 1954

After 24 wickets had fallen on day one of the County Championship match between Surrey and Northamptonshire at the Town Ground in Kettering, the hosts recovered to post 133 in the second innings, despite Jim Laker's 5-36. This left Surrey requiring 138 for victory, a total that looked far off at 102/7. However, having already taken 11 wickets in the match, Laker became a hero with the bat as well, hanging on to make 33* and guiding Surrey to the tightest of one-wicket victories.

5th AUGUST 1999

On 60* overnight, Alistair Brown carried on his innings in the County Championship match against Glamorgan at The Oval to reach 124 and help Surrey post a total of 309 all out. With wicketkeeper Jonathan Batty unable to take the field for the second innings, Brown then took the gloves and took two catches and made his only career stumping as Surrey rolled Glamorgan over for just 84, Saqlain Mushtaq taking 5-18.

6th AUGUST 1969

Bob Willis, a young fast bowler from Stoke d'Abernon, completed his journey to the Surrey first team when he made his debut in a three-day match against Scotland at The Oval. Willis enjoyed a quiet first day in the dressing room, watching first Micky Stewart and then Stewart Storey score centuries. On days two and three he would serve notice of his potential, taking 3-13 and 2-37 as Surrey won by an innings and 97 runs.

7th AUGUST 1997

The Hollioake brothers – Adam and Ben – made their Test debuts against Australia at Trent Bridge. Ben, at 19 years and 269 days, was the youngest England Test debutant since Brian Close in 1949 and the pair were the first brothers to play for England since 1957. It was a chastening first day for them though, spent entirely in the field as Australia moved up to 302/3. However in a memorable moment England captain Michael Atherton briefly bowled the two in tandem – up against the Australian batting pair of fellow brothers, Steve and Mark Waugh, who sadly got the upper hand.

8th AUGUST 1981

A County Championship match against Gloucestershire at Cheltenham College saw the start of something great for Surrey when a young wicketkeeper – the son of a club legend – made his first-class debut for the club. Alec Stewart was listed at number nine by captain Roger Knight but spent much of his first day in the profession watching the rain fall. The game ended in an eight-wicket defeat with Stewart making modest totals of two and eight and taking three catches. That was the end of his first-class adventure for 1981 and, after one more game in 1982, he made his breakthrough in 1983 and never looked back.

8th AUGUST 1995

Surrey suffered their biggest ever defeat in one-day cricket against the touring Young Australia team at The Oval. Facing a side that contained Matthew Hayden, Stuart Law, Ricky Ponting, Justin Langer, Adam Gilchrist and

Michael Kasprowicz, Surrey conceded 322/6 before responding with 143 all out with a makeshift team because of an injury crisis. The game is also notable for being the only Surrey first-team appearance for Gareth Townsend, who now plays a key role for the club as director of the Pemberton Greenish Surrey Academy. Although part of a hiding, Townsend took a catch and made ten from 31 balls before being caught behind.

9th AUGUST 1991

The late great Brian Johnston, ably accompanied by Jonathan Agnew, caused national hysteria when broadcasting from the Broadcasting Centre at The Oval during the fifth Test between England and the West Indies. Ian Botham, recalled for his first Test in two years, had been trying to take evasive action against Curtly Ambrose and in doing so attempted to swing his leg above his wicket, just failing to get sufficient clearance and being given out hit wicket. When summarising the incident on BBC radio at the end of the day's play, Agnew explained that Botham 'didn't quite get his leg over', causing him to dissolve into fits of infectious giggles. Johnston attempted to continue but became caught up in his colleague's laughter, uttering the unforgettable phrase 'oh Aggers, do stop it!' before collapsing himself and leaving cricket fans across the world listening to two grown men in peals of laughter.

9th AUGUST 1994

Surrey played Worcestershire in the semi-final of the NatWest Trophy at The Oval and conceded 357/2, including 180* from the Australian Tom Moody. Although Surrey got close and only lost by seven runs, Moody's innings remains the largest one-day score ever made against the club.

9th AUGUST 2000

Surrey played their first match at Whitgift School in Croydon – a picturesque venue distinguished by the two albino wallabies kept in the school's private zoo – a National League Division Two game against Warwickshire. Despite only making 211/9 from their 45 overs a virtuoso bowling display saw Adam Hollioake's side dismiss the opposition for just 108 to win by 103 runs.

10th AUGUST 1967

Surrey fast bowler Geoff Arnold made his Test debut – against Pakistan at Trent Bridge. 'Horse', as he is widely known, made a great start at the highest level, taking 3-35 as Pakistan were bowled out for 140. The match also saw the debut of great England wicketkeeper Alan Knott, who helped Arnold dismiss his soon to be county colleague Intikhab Alam for a duck.

10th AUGUST 1990

The Oval staged a one-day youth international match between Pakistan and England. The game featured such future luminaries as Moin Khan, John Crawley, Ronnie Irani, Darren Gough and Dominic Cork, and was won by Pakistan by 23 runs.

10th AUGUST 1991

Phil Tufnell produced one of the great modern-day performances at The Oval when he spun out the West Indies for just 176. 'Tuffers' took 6-25 and had the last five West Indian wickets for just 16 runs, including Viv Richards, who had been hoping for a glorious farewell to one of his happiest hunting grounds. England went on to win by five wickets to secure one of the most famous drawn series of all time. Tufnell was not named Man of the Match though, the honour going to Robin Smith, for one of his finest hundreds in the England first innings.

11th AUGUST 1870

One of the club's all-time greats, Tom Richardson, was born in Byfleet. Arguably the greatest bowler of the 19th century, Richardson took a club record 1,775 wickets at 17.87 during 305 appearances as well as a further 88 for England at 25.22.

11th AUGUST 1891

Surrey won their second County Championship after beating Gloucestershire at Bristol. George Lohmann took 11 wickets in the game, dismissing W.G. Grace in the first innings as Surrey won by ten wickets inside two days. By the end of the season, Surrey had more than double the points total of Lancashire in second place and had won 12 of their 16 games, only losing two.

11th AUGUST 1888

Surrey recorded their biggest innings victory when they defeated Sussex by an innings and 485 runs at The Oval. Centuries from Walter Read and Monty Bowden helped a side led by John Shuter to 698 all out. In response, Sussex could only manage totals of 114 and 99 with George Lohmann taking 12 wickets in the match.

11th AUGUST 1899

Having conceded 704 to Yorkshire, Tom Hayward and Bobby Abel set about repairing the damage in Surrey's first innings. The two came together on 58/3 and were not parted for the next 448 runs. They ended

11th August with Surrey on 169/3 and were eventually broken late on day three with the score at 506/4. Hayward hit 273 and Abel 193 as the two recorded what still remains the biggest partnership in club history. Unsurprisingly, the game at The Oval was drawn with Surrey left on 551/7.

11th AUGUST 1928

The West Indies made their first visit to The Oval for the third Test of the series against England. Sadly for the tourists, captained by Karl Nunes, the result in Kennington was no different to that in Manchester or St John's Wood with Percy Chapman's side winning by an innings. The game was also notable for Jack Hobbs's 159, his second, and largest, Test century at his home ground.

11th AUGUST 1930

Surrey recorded their biggest victory over Middlesex when they won a County Championship match at The Oval by an innings and 171 runs. Surrey opened with 419/8, thanks to 158 from Andy Sandham, and then rolled Middlesex for 125 and 123 with Alf Gover taking 6-48 in the first innings and Maurice Allom 5-43 in the second.

12th AUGUST 1896

England won the Ashes at The Oval with a 66-run victory over Australia that secured a 2-1 series triumph. In a very low-scoring game, England scored 145 and 84 but were able to keep Australia to 119 and 44. Surrey's Bobby Abel, Tom Hayward and Tom Richardson all played in the game.

12th AUGUST 1947

Denis Compton completed the unusual feat of scoring 100 runs and taking more than ten wickets in the match against Surrey at The Oval. Compton scored 137* in the first innings before taking 6-94 and 6-80 with his slow left-arm 'Chinaman' deliveries as Middlesex won by an innings and 11 runs.

12th AUGUST 1954

Pakistan made their first visit to The Oval, beating England by 24 runs and therefore securing a drawn series. The victory was earned on the back of fast bowler Fazal Mahmood who took match figures of 12-99 as England were twice bowled out for less than 150. The game was also notable as the Test debut of Surrey's Peter Loader, who played alongside his club-mate Peter May and took 3-35 in the first innings.

13th AUGUST 1884

England won the Ashes for the first time at The Oval. The urn was created for the 1882/83 series in Australia, won by England, and a drawn match here was enough to complete a 1-0 series win. The game will also be remembered for Surrey's Walter Read scoring 117 from number ten, an innings that still stands as the highest score by a number ten batsman in Test cricket.

13th AUGUST 1902

England beat Australia by one wicket at The Oval but still lost the series 2-1. This match is, allegedly, where Yorkshire pair George Hirst and Wilfred Rhodes – needing 15 to win – agreed to 'get 'em in singles'. However, to spoil a famous story, neither party could later remember using the phrase and Rhodes (who batted at number 11) even scored a boundary during the partnership.

13th AUGUST 1912

Sydney Barnes took 8-29 as England beat South Africa at The Oval to secure a 3-0 series win. Barnes's figures were the best at the ground for 82 years until Devon Malcolm bettered them, against the same opposition, with 9-57 in 1994.

13th AUGUST 1945

Robin David Jackman was born in Simla in India. Jackman made his first-class debut in 1966 and remains one of the most popular players to ever don the Surrey feathers. His 1,206 wickets for Surrey were taken with a combination of rare skill, raw aggression and superb belligerence and the fact he was only ever selected for four Test matches was of great benefit to the club, if frustrating for himself and his many fans. Jackman always spent a great deal of time in South Africa and, in retirement, established himself as one of the leading cricket commentators in the world, being largely employed by South African network SuperSport.

13th AUGUST 1996

Alec Stewart carried his bat throughout the NatWest Trophy semi-final against Essex to score 125 – his fourth one-day century of the season, a joint club record alongside Alistair Brown in 2001. Despite Stewart's heroics, Essex overturned Surrey's 275/5 and won the match by four wickets.

W.W. READ.
SURREY

SURREY'S WALTER READ, WHO SCORED A CENTURY WHEN ENGLAND WON THE ASHES AT THE OVAL FOR THE FIRST EVER TIME

13th AUGUST 2000

Surrey started the first County Championship match at Whitgift School, against Nottinghamshire. A brilliant 279* from Mark Ramprakash was the highlight as Surrey romped to victory by an innings and 211 runs. In the Surrey innings, the last two wickets gave up 236 runs with Ian Salisbury adding 65 and Saqlain Mushtaq 50 alongside Ramprakash.

14th AUGUST 1886

England beat Australia at The Oval by an innings and 217 runs to complete a 3-0 series win and retain the Ashes for the fourth consecutive series. England scored 434, with W.G. Grace making 170, and then dismissed Australia for 68 and 149, Surrey's George Lohmann taking match figures of 12-104.

14th AUGUST 1948

The man many consider to be the greatest batsman to ever play the game, Sir Donald Bradman, played his final innings at The Oval. In what was known to be his last game, Bradman required just four runs in either innings to secure the unthinkable, a Test average of 100. With England dismissed for just 52 and Australia already in a commanding position on 117/1, Bradman came to the crease in failing light shortly before 6pm on the first day. He was accompanied by a standing ovation from all in the crowd and was then given 'three cheers' by the England players. Clearly touched by this ovation, Bradman successfully defended his first ball from spinner Eric Hollies but played forward to his second and was clean bowled for a duck. When England were dismissed for just 188 in the second innings, Australia had won by an innings and 149 runs and Bradman was robbed of the chance to score the runs in the second innings. In later years, Bradman's poor luck in facing the relatively unheralded Hollies became clear as, when asked in an interview how he would have bowled to Bradman in that situation, Alec Bedser – the only Surrey player to appear in the match – said he would have allowed him to hit the required boundary. 'We had lost the series hopelessly already, what did it matter?' he told the BBC in 2008. 'It matters a lot now though, no one else will do it.'

14th AUGUST 1994

David Ward hit 87 as Surrey beat Essex by six wickets in an AXA Equity and Law League match at Castle Park Cricket Ground in Colchester. Ward's innings made him the only batsman in the history of the club to score ten one-day fifties in a single season. Despite this fine achievement, he is still only placed third in the one-day averages behind Graham Thorpe and Darren Bicknell.

15th AUGUST 1870

Surrey dismissed Kent for just 20 in a county match at The Oval, the second lowest total ever recorded against the club. The wickets were shared between James Southerton (5-16) and Walter Anstead (4-3).

15th AUGUST 1936

India played their first Test at The Oval, a nine-wicket defeat that gave England a 2-0 series win. Wally Hammond's 217 had set the match up for England before Jim Sims and Gubby Allen took 12 wickets between them to secure the victory.

15th AUGUST 1964

Fred Trueman became the first man to take 300 Test wickets when he dismissed Neil Hawke in the Australian first innings. Trueman had the considerable fortune that John Arlott was commentating for the BBC at the time, who famously observed: 'Neil Hawke can never have come into the Pavilion to a greater ovation in his life but they weren't looking at him!' Interviewed later by the Australian Alan McGilvray, the famously short-tempered Yorkshireman said that afterwards he 'felt like a child with a new birthday present...it was a wonderful feeling'.

15th AUGUST 1972

Pat Pocock, in the course of taking 7-67 against Sussex at Eastbourne, claimed four wickets in consecutive balls. After his fifth went for a single, Pocock then made it five wickets in an over as Surrey somehow scraped a draw. With three overs of the match left, Sussex were on 187/1, needing 204 to win. Pocock's penultimate over went for two runs and contained three wickets before his final over saw five wickets fall for just the one run. Sussex ended two runs short – but also with only one wicket in hand.

15th AUGUST 1987

Surrey wicketkeeper Jack Richards combined with Keith Medleycott to put on 262 for the seventh wicket during a County Championship game against Kent at The Oval. The partnership remains a record for Surrey for the seventh wicket.

16th AUGUST 1905

England drew with Australia at The Oval to complete a 2-0 series victory and retain the Ashes. England batted first and posted 430 all out. After the tourists replied with 363, England eventually set Australia 329 to win but they ended on 124/4 to secure the draw.

16th AUGUST 1957

Surrey won their 14th County Championship – and sixth in a row – when they beat Somerset at Weston-super-Mare. After an even first innings, Jim Laker's 6-66 left Surrey needing 153 which they reached with a top score of 32 from Ken Barrington. Surrey eventually won the title by 94 points from Nottinghamshire, winning 21 of 28 games.

16th AUGUST 1972

England lost a six-day Test to Australia at The Oval by five wickets to leave the series drawn at 2-2 – but still retained the Ashes due to their victory in Australia in 1970/71. Greg and Ian Chappell scored centuries and Dennis Lillee took ten wickets in the match as Australia scored 242 in the final innings.

16th AUGUST 2000

Gary Butcher completed a first-class hat-trick at The Oval when he dismissed Derbyshire's Paul Aldred, Tim Munton and Kevin Dean. Despite only making 260 in their first innings, Surrey won by an innings and 45 runs when Derbyshire managed just 97 in their second innings.

17th AUGUST 1871

Spin bowler James Southerton delivered a club record 476 balls during the first innings of Surrey's county match with Gloucestershire at Clifton College Close Ground in Clifton. Southerton got through 119 four-ball overs during Gloucestershire's 400, which took 251 overs and led them to an innings victory.

17th AUGUST 1928

Wally Hammond took six catches in the second innings for Gloucestershire in a County Championship match at The Oval. The haul is a record against Surrey and complemented the four Hammond had already taken in the first innings as Gloucestershire won by 189 runs.

17th AUGUST 1976

Michael Holding completed match figures of 14-149 for the West Indies against England as the tourists finished off a 3-0 series victory with a 231-run win. After Viv Richards's brilliant 291 in the first innings, Holding took 8-92 and 6-57 as not even 203 from Dennis Amiss could save England.

18th AUGUST 1926

England beat Australia by 289 runs to complete a tense 1-0 series win and regain the Ashes. Having drawn the first four Tests, England conceded a 22-run lead after the first innings but 100 from Jack Hobbs and 172 from Herbert Sutcliffe helped them set the tourists a massive 415 to win, a total they could not get close to thanks to Harold Larwood (3-34) and Wilfred Rhodes (4-44).

18th AUGUST 1934

Bill Ponsford and Don Bradman put on a partnership of 451 – the highest ever Test stand at The Oval – for the second wicket. Australia won the toss and batted first and, when Bill Brown went early to Nobby Clark, Ponsford and Bradman batted all day. Bradman went just before the close for 244 but Ponsford continued into the second day, eventually scoring 266 as Australia racked up 701 all out and went on to win by 562 runs, finishing a 2-1 series win and regaining the Ashes after losing them in controversial fashion during the 1932/33 'Bodyline' series in Australia.

18th AUGUST 1982

Middlesex recorded their lowest one-day total against Surrey during the NatWest Trophy semi-final. Replying to Surrey's 205/9, they were all out for just 80, with Sylvester Clarke taking 4-10 and Robin Jackman and Graham Monkhouse also taking three wickets each.

18th AUGUST 1994

South Africa started their first Test at The Oval since the end of the international sporting ban due to the country's apartheid regime. They had a strong first day, progressing solidly to 326/8 behind 93 from Brian McMillan, who was unbeaten on 91 overnight.

19th AUGUST 1898

Tom Hayward became the second man to hit more than 300 in an innings for Surrey when he managed 315* against Lancashire at The Oval. Hayward ended the first day on 163* but continued in the same vein the following day, only stopping when he ran out of partners with Surrey all out for 634. Sadly for Hayward, his mammoth effort was not in a winning cause with the game ending in a draw.

19th AUGUST 1907

South Africa became the first country other than Australia to play against England at The Oval, when they drew the final Test in a 1-0 series defeat.

England had a good start but some solid batting from Tip Snooke and Aubrey Faulkner saw the three-day match finish in a draw. Surrey trio Tom Hayward, Jack Crawford and Neville Knox featured in the game – with Hayward being dismissed lbw from the first ball of the match.

19th AUGUST 1953

England regained the Ashes at The Oval when they beat Australia by eight wickets in the final Test to secure a 1-0 series victory. Surrey trio Alec Bedser, Tony Lock and Jim Laker combined well to keep the visitors to 275 all out in the first innings and Peter May then scored 39 as England replied with 306. The game was tightly poised but 5-45 from Lock and 4-75 from Laker blew Australia away and they were all out for just 162 in the second innings. Chasing down a potentially slippery 132 to win back possession of the treasured urn, Peter May made a mature 37 to help England home.

19th AUGUST 1993

Adam Hollioake made his first-class debut for Surrey at the Rutland Recreation Ground in Ilkeston in a County Championship match that Surrey lost to Derbyshire by six wickets. His first day was not one to remember though, as he was dismissed by Alan Warner for 13 and then toiled fruitlessly with the ball as Derbyshire ended 106/0. The game would improve for him however, with the future club captain hitting a brilliant 123 in the second innings.

20th AUGUST 1938

Yorkshireman Len Hutton walked out in the shadow of the gasholders and embarked on one of the greatest feats of batting ever seen by an Englishman. Playing against an excellent Australian side led by Don Bradman, Hutton batted all day to finish on 160*. After a rest day in the middle, Hutton returned and continued to bat all day on day two, reaching exactly 300* at the end. He then continued on to a third day and was eventually caught by Lindsay Hassett off Bill O'Reilly for 364. His score remains the highest by an Englishman in Test cricket and the sixth-highest of all time.

20th AUGUST 1963

Peter Loader finished his last game for Surrey, against Essex at Clacton-on-Sea. The match was drawn but Loader went out on top personally, taking 4-58 in the first innings.

20th AUGUST 1994

Devon Malcolm, allegedly riled after hearing the South African slip cordon laugh when he was struck on the head by a Fanie de Villiers bouncer, turned around and promised that 'you guys are history'. Later in the day he ripped up the record books as he blew through the tourists' batting to take 9/57. The figures remain the best in Tests at The Oval and are only bettered on the all-time list for England by Jim Laker's twin efforts at Old Trafford in 1956.

20th AUGUST 2001

Mark Butcher played one of the finest innings by any Surrey batsman when he hit an unbeaten 173 against Australia at Headingley. The tourists, boasting an attack featuring a peak Sharne Warne, Brett Lee and Glenn McGrath, had already taken an unassailable 3-0 lead. They had set England 315 to win on the final day and when Michael Atherton fell to McGrath early, it seemed the wheels had been set in motion. However Butcher – showing the tenacity and ability that Surrey fans had always known – batted throughout the day, getting support from Nasser Hussain and Mark Ramprakash to end on a Test best 173*, lead England to a famous six-wicket victory and prevent a humiliating 5-0 'greenwash'.

20th AUGUST 2006

The fourth Test between England and Pakistan at The Oval ended amid farcical scenes when Pakistan were accused by umpire Darrell Hair of tampering with the ball and penalised five runs. After tea on the fourth day a stand-off ensued between Pakistan and Hair and the game was officially ended and awarded to England. The final result has since been subject to a number of appeals and was most recently awarded – in 2009 – to England.

21st AUGUST 1845

A two-day game between the Gentlemen of Surrey and the Players of Surrey was played at The Oval. After the match, which was drawn, a dinner was held at the nearby Horns Tavern – situated on Kennington Lane, opposite what is now a branch of Barclays Bank – to discuss the formation of a Surrey County Cricket Club. The Horns Tavern itself was rebuilt in 1887, suffered bomb damage in the Second World War and was finally demolished in the 1960s.

21st AUGUST 1931

Andy Ducat played his last game for Surrey, against Somerset at Taunton. Sadly for Ducat, the game was badly affected by the weather and he was not given a chance to play one final innings.

22nd AUGUST 1890

Surrey won the first official County Championship when Kent failed to beat Lancashire at Beckenham. At the time, Surrey were in the midst of losing a tight match to Yorkshire at The Oval but – with the points system of the time awarding one for a win and taking one away for a loss – Surrey's minimum possible tally of six points was mathematically unbeatable and the club had won their first trophy, in their 44th year of existence.

22nd AUGUST 1892

Surrey and England great Percy Fender was born in Balham. Fender was a controversial but often brilliant figure at Surrey and led the club from 1920 to 1931. Through a rocky relationship with the game's authorities, he only played 13 Tests, to limited success, and died in June 1985.

22nd AUGUST 1939

Eddie Watts became the third man to take all ten wickets in an innings for Surrey when he single-handedly bowled out Warwickshire at Edgbaston. Watts, a popular and hard-working right-arm fast bowler, achieved the feat in the second innings, taking 10-67 as Surrey won by an innings and one run.

22nd AUGUST 1952

Surrey won their ninth County Championship – and first in the unmatched streak of seven in a row – when they beat Derbyshire at The Oval by 212 runs. As so often in that period, Surrey could thank Tony Lock for his 6-16 in the Derbyshire first innings before 88 from Peter May and four wickets for Alec Bedser in the visitors' second innings finished the job. Surrey eventually won the title by 32 points from Yorkshire, winning 20 of their 28 games.

22nd AUGUST 1957

Test Match Special was broadcast from The Oval for the very first time, providing ball-by-ball commentary on the final Test between England and the West Indies.

DEVON MALCOLM WALKS OFF WITH FIGURES OF 9-57 AGAINST SOUTH AFRICA AT THE OVAL IN 1994

22nd AUGUST 2011

Surrey announced the signing of Indian left-arm spinner Pragyan Ojha for the end of the season. Signed to help Surrey achieve promotion back to the top flight, Ojha was a spectacular success. He took 24 wickets at an average of 12.95 – including 6-8 against fellow promotion contenders Northamptonshire – helping Surrey to big wins in their last four games.

23rd AUGUST 1972

Mark Alan Butcher was born in Croydon, a son to Surrey opener and future coach Alan and eventual older brother to another Surrey player, Gary. Butcher made his debut for Surrey in 1992 and went on to become a key part of one the most successful eras in club history. He played 182 times for Surrey, scoring 12,181 runs at 44.45 and also played in 71 Tests, scoring a further 4,288 runs. He captained Surrey from 2005 to 2009, leading them to the Division Two title and promotion to Division One in 2006.

23rd AUGUST 2009

England won back the Ashes at The Oval when they beat Australia by 197 runs. After an even start, the game turned during a brilliant spell by Stuart Broad on the second day, with England solidifying their advantage through a hundred from debutant Jonathan Trott. Chasing 546 to win, Australia were bowled out late on day four, when Graeme Swann forced Mike Hussey to prod to Alastair Cook at short leg.

24th AUGUST 1854

Surrey played their only game at Broadwater Park, Godalming. The three-day match saw a 65-run victory over Nottinghamshire.

24th AUGUST 1904

Bobby Abel played his last game of cricket against Somerset at Taunton. Abel scored only nine in the first innings and came in at number ten for his final time at the crease, being given lbw to Ernie Robson.

24th AUGUST 1938

Following Len Hutton's incredible innings over the first three days, England recorded what is still the largest win in Test history over Australia. Replying to England's 903/7 declared, Australia – without Don Bradman after he injured an ankle fielding – posted just 201 and then 123 to lose by an innings and 579 runs.

25th AUGUST 1895

Surrey won their fourth County Championship when they beat Sussex by an innings and 15 runs at Hove. The victory was largely thanks to the brilliance of Bill Lockwood and Tom Richardson, who between them took 19 of the 20 wickets to fall. Surrey won the title by a single point from Yorkshire and won 13 of their 16 games.

25th AUGUST 1945

Surrey played their only match at Cambridge Avenue, New Malden, an official wartime game against Sussex, who featured future Surrey captain Stuart Surridge in their side. Surrey bowled Sussex out for 76 and reached the total for the loss of six wickets.

25th AUGUST 1954

Surrey began an extraordinary match at The Oval against Worcestershire. The game remains a club record today for the lowest aggregate of runs collectively scored. After bowling out the visitors for just 25, Stuart Surridge declared Surrey's innings closed on 92/3 before Surrey returned and bowled Worcestershire out again, this time for just 40. The total number of runs scored was just 157.

26th AUGUST 1902

Robert James 'Bob' Gregory was born in Selsdon. Gregory made his debut for Surrey in 1925 and played for the club until 1947, playing 413 times despite missing five full seasons due to the Second World War. During this time he made 18,978 runs for the club at an average of 34.75 as well as taking 434 wickets at an average of 31.97. He died in 1973, aged 71, in Wandsworth.

26th AUGUST 1954

Surrey won their 11th County Championship – and third consecutive – when they beat Worcestershire by an innings and 27 runs at The Oval. The details of the extraordinary match are reported in the entry for 25th August. Surrey eventually won the title by 22 points from Yorkshire, winning 15 of their 28 games

26th AUGUST 1955

Surrey won their 12th County Championship – and fourth consecutive – when they beat Sussex at The Oval by an innings and eight runs. Runs from Bernard Constable and Arthur McIntyre helped Surrey to a 98-run lead on the first innings before 5-41 from Alec Bedser and match figures of 9-106 from Tony Lock secured the win. Surrey eventually won the title by 16 points from Yorkshire, winning 23 of their 28 games.

27th AUGUST 1892

Surrey won their third County Championship – and third in a row – when Nottinghamshire lost to Lancashire at Old Trafford. The day before, Surrey had completed a ten-wicket win over Kent at The Oval and they eventually won the title by three points from Nottinghamshire, winning 13 of their 16 games.

27th AUGUST 1998

Sri Lanka started their first Test at The Oval, a ten-wicket victory over England in the only match of the series. Despite England's John Crawley-inspired 445, Sri Lanka hit back with Sanath Jayasuriya firing 213 and Aravinda de Silva 152. When the brilliant Muttiah Muralitharan ripped through England to take 9-65 and complete match figures of 16-220 – an all-time Test record at The Oval – the tourists required just 36 to win.

27th AUGUST 2002

Surrey started a County Championship game against Warwickshire at Edgbaston that was eventually drawn. As well as centuries for Ian Ward and Nadeem Shahid the game was notable for the club record 552 deliveries sent down by spinner Saqlain Mushtaq.

28th AUGUST 1956

England drew with Australia at The Oval to complete a 2-1 series victory and retain the Ashes for the third consecutive series. With Australia only able to retain pride with a drawn series, this very rainy affair was not one of the great Tests played at the ground.

29th AUGUST 1882

England lost to Australia at The Oval – a result considered so shocking to the assembled crowds that the *Sporting Times* published an obituary to the English game saying that 'the body will be cremated and the ashes taken to Australia'. Legend holds that the bails used in the match were taken away by a group of women and burnt before being placed into an urn that was presented to England captain Ivo Bligh on England's next tour of Australia the following winter. The game itself was a very memorable one with the 'demon bowler' Frederick Spofforth taking 7-44 in the final innings as England, chasing just 85 to win, came up seven short.

29th AUGUST 1952

Laurie Fishlock played his last game for Surrey, a draw against Northamptonshire at The Oval. Fishlock hit 39 in the first innings and ended 19* in the second.

29th AUGUST 1972

Micky Stewart finished his last match for Surrey – a 21-run victory over Nottinghamshire at The Oval. Captaining the side, Stewart hit 24 in the first innings and three in the second as a five-wicket haul from Pat Pocock caused Nottinghamshire to finish just short of their target.

30th AUGUST 1926

During a County Championship game against Middlesex at Lord's, Jack Hobbs hit his personal best score of 316*, becoming the fourth player to complete the achievement for the club. Hobbs had started his innings two days before, reaching 256* overnight before benefitting from a rest day. He came back refreshed and continued on before captain Percy Fender declared the innings closed on 579/5. In the end, Surrey won the game by an innings and 63 runs.

30th AUGUST 1935

Percy Fender played his last game for Surrey, a draw against Middlesex at Lord's. Fender took 4-103 in the first innings and 1-49 in the second as well as scoring 44. As the game ended he was 5* in the second innings.

30th AUGUST 1960

Alec Bedser finished his last game for Surrey, a win over Glamorgan by an innings and 77 runs. Bedser took 5-25 in the first innings and 0-15 in the second. In one of the very few instances of their lives not running symmetrically, Alec's twin Eric decided to play on for a further year.

30th AUGUST 1977

England drew with Australia to win back the Ashes with a 3-0 series victory. Although Australia had the advantage there was always little chance of a result after the first day and a large part of the third were entirely lost to rain.

31st AUGUST 1939

Surrey captain Monty Garland-Wells and Lancashire skipper Thomas Higson agreed to end their ongoing County Championship match at The Oval as a draw due to the outbreak of war.

31st AUGUST 1946

Surrey started their inaugural first-class match at the Leyland Motors Ground in Kingston-upon-Thames, a draw with Hampshire. The game featured one of the most bizarre dismissals seen in a Surrey match when Alf Gover caught Rodney Exton off the bowling of Jim Laker. Gover – who had just finished bowling an over – was still putting on his jumper at short leg when Exton played Laker into the leg side. Despite being blinded by his jumper, Gover felt the ball come towards him and instinctively clasped his legs together. The ball lodged between his thighs and Exton was out.

31st AUGUST 1956

Surrey won their 13th County Championship – and fifth in a row – when they drew with Lancashire at The Oval. The match was a rain-ruined affair, with no play possible on the final two days, but saw Surrey clinch another championship. They eventually won the title from Lancashire by 20 points, winning 15 of their 28 matches.

31st AUGUST 1962

Wicketkeeper Arnold Long ended the season with a club record 91 victims in a season. Long managed to beat the previous best – 87 by Fred Stedman in 1901 – despite only taking one catch in the final game against Hampshire at Southampton.

31st AUGUST 2004

Adam Hollioake played his last game for Surrey, a 48-run defeat to Lancashire in the totesport League Division One. Hollioake scored 12 and took 0-27 from three overs. The date is also another landmark for Hollioake, who played his first game for England – a one-day international against Pakistan at Edgbaston – on 31st August 1996, in which he scored 15 and took 4-23 as England won by 107 runs.

31st AUGUST 2010

Surrey announced they had signed Kevin Pietersen on loan from Hampshire until the end of the season. Pietersen had been omitted from the England squad for a one-day international and Twenty20 series against Pakistan and would eventually sign for the club full-time ahead of the 2011 season.

SURREY CCC
On This Day

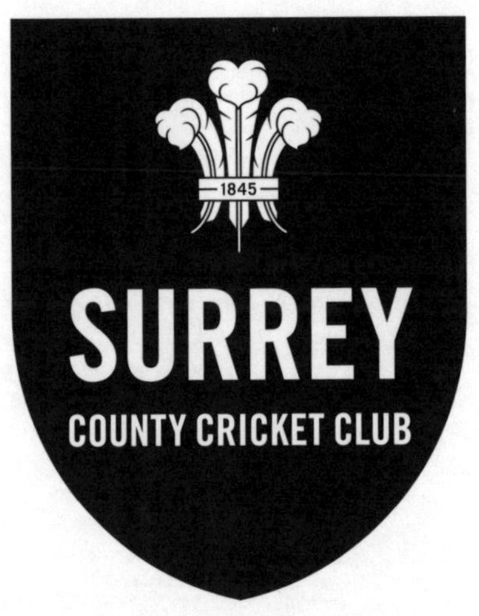

SEPTEMBER

1st SEPTEMBER 1914

Tom Hayward played his last game for Surrey, a big County Championship victory over Gloucestershire at The Oval. Hayward only managed one run but centuries from Jack Hobbs and Donald Knight helped Surrey to 400 before Gloucestershire fell first for 100 and then for 264 with nine wickets for Percy Fender and seven for Bill Hitch.

1st SEPTEMBER 1950

Surrey won their eighth County Championship – awarded jointly with Lancashire – after beating Leicestershire by ten wickets at The Oval with 8-53 from Alec Bedser and 108 from Laurie Fishlock. Both teams finished on 220 points, although Lancashire won 17 of their 28 games to Surrey's 16.

1st SEPTEMBER 1953

Surrey won their tenth County Championship – and second in a row – when they drew with Sussex at Hove. After conceding a one-run deficit following the first innings, 136* from Peter May in the second saw Surrey cruise to 244/2 and the required draw. The title was won by 16 points from Sussex, with Surrey winning 13 of their 28 games.

1st SEPTEMBER 1981

England wrapped up a 3-1 series victory by drawing with Australia at The Oval and retained the Ashes. After conceding a small lead after the first innings, Australia scored 344/9 declared, setting England 383 to win. They looked briefly in trouble when Ian Botham was dismissed for 16 but a stabilising 70* from Alan Knott saw them through to the draw.

2nd SEPTEMBER 1896

George Lohmann walked off the field as a Surrey player for the final time having taken 11 wickets in the match to give Surrey a ten-wicket victory over Sussex at Hove.

2nd SEPTEMBER 1911

Surrey fell to their biggest defeat against Middlesex, losing by 353 runs at Lord's, a game in which Jack Hearne took match figures of 15-122.

2nd SEPTEMBER 1947

Alf Gover played his last game for Surrey, a victory by an innings and 73 runs over Somerset at Taunton. Gover contributed six wickets to the win, which was set up by the unusual feat of Alec Bedser's only ever career hundred – 126, scored from number nine.

2nd SEPTEMBER 1981

Christopher Timothy Tremlett was born in Southampton, the third generation of a Hampshire cricketing dynasty that started with Maurice and continued with his son Tim. One of the most dangerous English fast bowlers of the last ten years, Tremlett has had an injury-plagued career and made the move from Hampshire to Surrey in 2010 to give himself a fresh start. The idea worked very well as he quickly bowled his way back into international contention and played a key role in England's victory in the 2010/11 Ashes.

2nd SEPTEMBER 1985

England dramatically regained the Ashes after an innings victory over Australia at The Oval saw them win the series 2-1. Although no one else in the side managed to score more than 20, 196 from opener Graham Gooch and 157 from ever-stylish captain David Gower saw England post a strong 464 all out before Australia were dismissed first for 241 and then just 129, with Richard Ellison taking 5-46 to secure victory by an innings and 94 runs. The win was duly celebrated by Ian Botham emptying a bottle of champagne over the head of his unsuspecting captain.

2nd SEPTEMBER 1999

Surrey won their 17th County Championship title when they beat Nottinghamshire by ten wickets at The Oval. After bowling the visitors out for 115 in the first innings, Surrey only posted 199 before bowling Nottinghamshire out for 233 in the second innings, with Saqlain Mushtaq and Ian Salisbury taking four wickets each. However, undaunted by needing 153 to win, Mark Butcher and Ian Ward calmly knocked off the runs without losing a wicket. Surrey eventually won the title by 55 points from Lancashire, winning 12 of 17 games.

3rd SEPTEMBER 1895

Surrey won their fifth title when they beat Hampshire by an innings at The Oval. Tom Richardson took 6-85 in the first innings as the visitors were 182 all out before 131 from opener Maurice Read helped Surrey to a dominant 374 all out. Richardson was in superb form again in the second innings, flying through the Hampshire batsmen to finish with 9-70 and match figures of 15-155. Surrey eventually won the title by three points from Lancashire, winning 17 of their 26 matches.

3rd SEPTEMBER 1917

Walter Stuart Surridge was born in Herne Hill. After making his debut for the club in 1947, Surridge was appointed captain in 1952, taking over from Michael Barton. Surrey won the County Championship in every year of his tenure before he retired from the game and handed over the leadership to Peter May. He played 254 matches for Surrey, taking 464 wickets at 29.64 but, most importantly, provided inspirational and canny leadership to one of the most talented squads ever assembled in the domestic game.

3rd SEPTEMBER 1937

Andy Sandham played his last game for Surrey, a seven-wicket victory over Sussex at Hove. Naturally, the effortlessly classy batsman went out on top, scoring 102 in the first innings.

3rd SEPTEMBER 1944

Geoffrey Graham Arnold, forever known as 'Horse' because of his initials G.G., was born in Earlsfield. A very fine fast bowler, Arnold took 745 wickets for Surrey at just 19.94, adding a further 115 in 34 Tests for England. Arnold left Surrey for Sussex in 1978, where he played out the final five seasons of his career. In retirement he returned to The Oval where he became first-team coach from 1986–1993, and bowling coach in 2003.

4th SEPTEMBER 1959

Jim Laker played his last game for Surrey, a four-wicket loss to Northamptonshire at Northampton. Uncharacteristically, Laker took just one wicket in the match, although his strike partner Tony Lock managed 5-107 in the second innings.

4th SEPTEMBER 1982

Surrey won the NatWest Trophy for the first time, beating Warwickshire by nine wickets at Lord's. Warwickshire were bowled out for just 158, with pace bowling trio Sylvester Clarke, Robin Jackman and David Thomas all bowling their allocation at less than two and a half runs an over. In response, Alan Butcher played superbly for his unbeaten 86 and received fine support from Geoff Howarth and David Smith as Surrey knocked off the runs with almost half of their overs remaining.

4th SEPTEMBER 1987

The great West Indian Sylvester Clarke took his career-best 8-62 for Surrey in a County Championship match against Northamptonshire at The Oval. Often unplayably quick – and benefitting from a wider mean streak than most – Clarke was feared by batsmen across the country and on this occasion bowled Surrey to a comfortable ten-wicket victory.

5th SEPTEMBER 1969

Mark Ravin Ramprakash was born in Bushey, Hertfordshire. After leaving Surrey's cross-capital rivals Middlesex for The Oval in 2001, 'Ramps' never looked back. He struck 61 first-class centuries for Surrey as part of his overall 15,837 runs at a staggering average of 67.96 – which comfortably outstrips Hobbs, Hayward, Sandham and Edrich, the four Surrey players he shares the feat of 100 first-class hundreds with.

5th SEPTEMBER 1971

Adam John Hollioake was born in Melbourne, Australia. After making his debut for the club in 1993, Hollioake's outstanding leadership qualities were recognised in 1997 when he became Surrey's 35th captain. During his seven-year reign, Surrey won three County Championship titles and five limited overs trophies.

6th SEPTEMBER 1880

The Oval staged the first Test match to be played in England, a five-wicket victory for Lord Harris's England side over Billy Murdoch's Australians. The highlights of the three-day match – played in front of a combined crowd of 44,428 – were centuries, made first by W.G. Grace (152) and then Murdoch himself (153). As the Ashes had yet to be created, they were not at stake.

6th SEPTEMBER 1899

Surrey won their sixth County Championship when they avoided defeat against Warwickshire at The Oval. Bill Lockwood took five wickets as Warwickshire were dismissed for 155 in their first innings before 94 from Bobby Abel, 137 from Tom Hayward and 76 from Lockwood saw Surrey to an unassailable 462/6. Although Surrey ended the year level on points with Middlesex, the large number of draws they achieved (14 out of 26 games) played in their favour as their percentage of points from games completed was higher than Middlesex and gave them the trophy for the first time in four years.

6th SEPTEMBER 1946

Roger David Verdon Knight was born in Streatham. After a long career for Cambridge University, Knight made his Surrey debut in 1968 and stayed at the club until 1970 when he moved to Gloucestershire. He then went to Sussex but came back to The Oval as captain in 1978, a position he held until 1983. During this time, Surrey finished runners-up on a number of occasions but went all the way in 1982, winning the NatWest Trophy. After his retirement a year later, Knight began a distinguished career in administration that led to him becoming first secretary and then chief executive of MCC, a member of the ECB Management Board and also president of Surrey CCC in 2008.

6th SEPTEMBER 1963

Tony Lock played his last match for Surrey, a drawn game with Warwickshire at The Oval. Sadly for the great left-arm spinner it was a rain-drenched affair with very little play possible. However, although he had finished with Surrey, he extended his career with a spell at Leicestershire from 1965 to 1967 and continued to play for Western Australia during the English winter.

6th SEPTEMBER 1968

Ken Barrington played his final match for Surrey, a drawn game with Hampshire at The Oval. It was not a fitting way for a player of his talent to bow out of the sport, with Barrington run out for a duck in the first innings and dismissed for just eight in the second.

6th SEPTEMBER 2006

Surrey won promotion back to Division One of the County Championship as winners of Division Two after a draw with Gloucestershire at Bristol. It was an excellent draw to secure as – set 500 to win the match – Surrey were 210/5. However, a great final afternoon fightback led by Stewart Walters and Chris Schofield, and completed by Nayan Doshi and Jade Dernbach, saw Surrey secure the nine points required. The title was eventually won by 22 points from second-placed Worcestershire.

7th SEPTEMBER 1932

Eugene 'Sir John' Paul Getty was born in the United States of America. The eldest son of John Paul Getty Snr – for a time one of the richest men in the world – he was known as a long-term anglophile and took British citizenship in 1997 after living an extraordinary life across the world. Supposedly introduced to the game of cricket by Mick Jagger of the Rolling Stones, Getty built an exact replica of The Oval's playing area in the grounds of his country estate at Wormsley in Herefordshire. He was appointed president of Surrey CCC in 1996 and sadly died in a London hospital, aged 70, in April 2003.

7th SEPTEMBER 1973

The Oval staged its first ever one-day international, only the ninth that had taken place, when England played the West Indies. It was an eight-wicket loss for an England side containing Surrey's Geoff Arnold.

THE GREAT TONY LOCK, WHO TOOK 1,713 WICKETS FOR SURREY

England managed just 189/9 and then saw Roy Fredericks hit 105 as the West Indies sauntered to victory.

7th SEPTEMBER 1978

John Edrich played his last game for Surrey, a ten-wicket defeat to Middlesex at The Oval. Edrich hit 29 in the first innings and 13 in the second.

7th SEPTEMBER 2002

Surrey won their 19th – and most recent – County Championship when Warwickshire failed to beat Lancashire at Old Trafford. Surrey still had two more games to play – subsequent victories over Hampshire and Leicestershire – and eventually won the title by 44.75 points, winning ten of their 16 matches that season.

8th SEPTEMBER 1990

Darren Bicknell and David Ward put on 413 for the third wicket in a County Championship match against Kent at the St Lawrence Ground in Canterbury. The game was eventually drawn but the partnership still stands as the largest for the third wicket in club history.

8th SEPTEMBER 2003

Alec Stewart played his last game of cricket, the fifth Test between England and South Africa at The Oval. England won the match by nine wickets to leave a superb series drawn at 2-2. Stewart scored 38 in the first innings and was not required to bat in the second. The Surrey and England legend was accompanied in the England team by three of his longest-serving team-mates and friends, Mark Butcher, Graham Thorpe and Martin Bicknell – who had been called up ten years after his last Test and was representing England on his home ground for the first time. As Stewart walked, triumphantly, from the pitch for the final time on home quarters he was warmly congratulated by his three team-mates.

9th SEPTEMBER 2001

Alistair Brown equalled Alec Stewart's club record of four one-day hundreds in a season when he hit 130 in Surrey's five-wicket win against Nottinghamshire at Trent Bridge in the Norwich Union League.

9th SEPTEMBER 2011

Alec Stewart was appointed to the board of Surrey CCC as executive director. Stewart had made his official 'return' to the club in 2009 and had been working on the coaching staff for three seasons but his new position gave him a very senior voice, with Surrey CCC chairman Richard Thompson likening Stewart's role to that held for many years by Bobby Charlton at Manchester United.

10th SEPTEMBER 2004

New Zealand recorded the biggest one-day international victory at The Oval when they beat the United States of America by 210 runs in a group match at the ICC Champions Trophy.

11th SEPTEMBER 1895

Tom Richardson walked off the field for the final time that summer having just helped A.E. Stoddart's XI to a 218-run victory over 'The Rest'. It had been an extraordinary season for the fast bowler, who had taken 252 wickets in the season over 27 matches at an average of just 13.94. Appropriately, his final act of the season was to take 5-21 in the last innings of the match, played at the Central Recreation Ground in Hastings.

11th SEPTEMBER 1956

Stuart Surridge played his last game for Surrey, a loss by 128 runs to 'The Rest'. Surrey had secured the County Championship on 31st August that summer, meaning they earned the right to play against an XI made up of the best players from all other counties. Surridge led the side but did not bowl himself as Surrey fell to a symbolic but meaningless defeat.

12th SEPTEMBER 1906

Tom Hayward laid down his bat for the final time in an extraordinary season that had seen him hit 3,246 runs in 32 matches at an average of 72.13. Hayward's final match was for 'The Rest' against county champions Kent and saw him hit 51 and 17 as his side won by 251 runs at The Oval.

12th SEPTEMBER 2005

England completed their victory in what many describe as the greatest series of all time – returning the Ashes to this country for the first time in 16 years. They had started the day by no means assured of the draw needed to complete a 2-1 series victory but a blazing 158 from a skunk-haired Kevin Pietersen – and a less well remembered 59 from Ashley Giles – saw parties go on late into the Kennington night. Days earlier, the ground had seen a very strange sight indeed as a crowd that could have been sold out five times over jokingly raised umbrellas and celebrated the fact there was no cricket to watch as they urged the weather gods to help England to the series.

13th SEPTEMBER 1957

The season ended when Surrey completed a six-wicket victory over 'The Rest' at Scarborough thanks to 136 from Ken Barrington and eight wickets from Tony Lock. The game also saw Micky Stewart take two more catches to up his total for the season to 77 – a club record for a fielder by 13 from Barrington, who took 64 in the same season.

13th SEPTEMBER 1969

Shane Keith Warne was born in Ferntree Gully, Victoria, Australia. Warne would grow up to become one of the greatest bowlers of all time, a tricky leg-spinner who took 1,319 first-class victims. He also holds the honour of being the leading overseas Test wicket-taker at The Oval, with 32 at 22.25.

13th SEPTEMBER 1971

Surrey won their 16th County Championship when they gained six bonus points in the final match of the season against Hampshire at Southampton. The game was lost by four wickets but Surrey ended joint top of the final table on 255 points with Warwickshire. Surrey had won 11 matches to Warwickshire's nine and the title came back to The Oval for the first time since 1958.

13th SEPTEMBER 2000

Surrey won their 18th County Championship when they secured their first bowling point against Lancashire at Old Trafford. The game was eventually drawn but the title had been secured on the first day when the point was gained. Surrey eventually finished 20 points clear of second-placed Lancashire, having won nine of their 16 games.

14th SEPTEMBER 1982

Robin Jackman played his last game for Surrey, a draw against Yorkshire. Jackman signed off for the club with 2-92 in the first innings and 0-22 in the second but walked off for the final time in a Surrey shirt holding a bat with his score on 40*. The game was not his final first-class outing though, as he was in the England CCC squad for the 1982/83 Australian tour and although he did not play a Test he played against state opposition and in one-day internationals.

15th SEPTEMBER 1910

Razor Smith walked off the field for the final time that season, having taken 225 first-class wickets. The off-spinner had added six to his tally by playing for 'The Rest' as they beat champions Kent at The Oval by 244 runs. He took his wickets at 12.83 in 32 matches and is the only bowler other than Tom Richardson to complete the feat for Surrey.

15th SEPTEMBER 1996

Surrey won the AXA Equity & Law League when they beat Glamorgan by seven wickets at Sophia Gardens in Cardiff. The Welshmen scored 159/9 from their 40 overs, a total Surrey sailed past with captain Alec Stewart scoring an unbeaten 41. Although they ended the 17-game season level on 50 points and 12 wins with Nottinghamshire, a hugely superior run rate of 16.1 saw Surrey awarded the trophy.

15th SEPTEMBER 2001

Ben Hollioake played his last game for Surrey, a drawn match with Glamorgan at Sophia Gardens. In a game dominated by Surrey's first innings of 701/9 declared, Hollioake took three wickets and scored 27 runs.

16th SEPTEMBER 1932

Michael James 'Micky' Stewart was born in 1932. One of the game's finest servants in this country, Stewart played 498 times for Surrey – leading the club from 1963 to 1972. During this time he scored 25,007 runs at 33.20 and took a club record 605 catches. After his retirement he served as cricket manager of Surrey from 1979 to 1986 and then England from 1986 to 1992. After that, he was appointed as ECB director of coaching from 1992 to 1997, where he was given credit for introducing many of the modern practices that have seen England become a very successful side. After retirement from this post, he served as Surrey president in 1998 and 1999 and is still involved with club and country today.

16th SEPTEMBER 1972

The Oval hosted 'Rock at The Oval', the second ever rock concert at the ground, headlined by prog rock titans Frank Zappa and Hawkwind.

16th SEPTEMBER 1986

Pat Pocock played his last game of cricket for Surrey, a 90-run victory over Leicestershire at The Oval. The fixture lost a great deal of time to the weather but Pocock and his fellow captain Peter Willey agreed that Leicestershire should chase 271 to win on the last day. Pocock took 3-66 in what was his final first-class appearance.

17th SEPTEMBER 2007

Surrey announced the release of 20-year-old Academy graduate Rory Hamilton-Brown. Speaking about the decision, coach Alan Butcher said: 'It's important that Surrey players really want to play for the club and this is why we have agreed with his request. We wish him the best of luck for his future endeavours.'

17th SEPTEMBER 2010

Umar Gul took 6-42 for Pakistan in a 23-run one-day international victory over England at The Oval. They are the best ODI figures ever taken at the ground.

17th SEPTEMBER 2011

Surrey won the Clydesdale Bank 40 with a five-wicket Duckworth-Lewis victory over Somerset at Lord's. Excellent bowling from Jade Dernbach had restricted the dangerous Somerset batsmen to just 214 all out and – with a reduced total on a showery afternoon at Lord's – skipper Rory Hamilton-Brown, now back at Surrey, hit a steadying innings of 78 as his side walked home with almost three overs to spare.

18th SEPTEMBER 1970

Darren Gough was born in Monk Bretton, Barnsley, Yorkshire. Often a fearsome adversary for Surrey, Gough also holds the record for playing in the most one-day internationals at The Oval, with 13.

18th SEPTEMBER 1971

The Oval staged its first rock concert when The Who headlined 'Goodbye Summer: A Concert for Bangladesh' with support from Rod Stewart's The Faces. In honour of the unique venue, Who drummer Keith Moon came on to stage brandishing a cricket bat which he proceeded to use throughout the first song, 'Summertime Blues'.

19th SEPTEMBER 2008

Surrey lost to Nottinghamshire at The Oval in Alan Butcher's final match as coach. Debutant Stuart Meaker formed part of a strong pace attack alongside the Pakistani Shoaib Akhtar but it was not enough to get through Nottinghamshire who piled on 532 before dismissing Surrey for 122 in their second innings to win by an innings and 143 runs. The result meant Surrey had gone through the summer without a first-class win and finished bottom of Division One with just 124 points.

THE LATE BEN HOLLIOAKE, A HUGELY TALENTED ALL-ROUNDER FOR SURREY AND ENGLAND WHOSE CAREER WAS CUT TRAGICALLY SHORT

20th SEPTEMBER 1993

Pakistani legend Waqar Younis played his last game for Surrey. The fast bowler spent three seasons at the club as a young man in 1990, 1991 and 1993. Sadly, his final match was totally ruined by rain, giving him no chance to add to the 232 wickets at 19.05 he had taken for Surrey.

21st SEPTEMBER 2002

Surrey completed their biggest runs victory when they ended the 2002 season by beating Leicestershire at The Oval. Ian Ward and Scott Newman scored hundreds in Surrey's first innings of 494 before 107 from Alistair Brown and a career best 208 from Adam Hollioake saw them amass another 492 in the second. When Tim Murtagh's 5-39 helped Leicestershire on their way to 142 all out, celebrations could commence. Not only had Surrey already been county champions for two weeks, they had just won a match by 483 runs.

22nd SEPTEMBER 2007

Although Surrey's future coach Chris Adams was still Sussex captain, he had great cause to thank his old adversary Mark Butcher as Butcher's Surrey side beat Lancashire to hand Sussex the title in a dramatic end to the domestic season. After twin tons from Mark Ramprakash had helped Surrey set Lancashire a giant 489 to win, a century from Indian V.V.S. Laxman and a strong combined team batting effort saw Mark Chilton's side inching towards their first title since they shared it with Surrey in 1950. However, when Dominic Cork was bowled by Murtaza Hussain, they had come up just 24 runs short and Adams's party started on the south coast.

23rd SEPTEMBER 2005

As they replied to Middlesex's challenging total of 404/5 declared during a County Championship match at The Oval, Surrey made their highest score against their old rivals, setting up a 282-run lead with 686/5. As ever, Mark Ramprakash enjoyed batting against his old employers with 252 and Azhar Mahmood also went big, hitting a career best 204*. They added 318 for the fifth wicket, not just a club record for the fifth wicket but a record for any wicket against Middlesex. The final day saw Middlesex capitulate for 243 and Surrey record the win by an innings and 39 runs, but Surrey had been relegated during the match.

24th SEPTEMBER 1946

Patrick Ian 'Percy' Pocock was born in Bangor, Caernarvonshire, Wales. Pocock was a great player for Surrey, from his debut in 1964 to his final match in 1986. He played 485 first-class matches and made a further 318 one-day appearances for Surrey, taking a combined total of 1,725 wickets for the club, and played 25 Tests and one one-day international for England.

25th SEPTEMBER 1922

Percy Fender walked off the field for the last time that campaign having completed the rare double of scoring 1,000 runs and taking 100 wickets in a season. Fender had just finished captaining the Royal Air Force to an eight-wicket victory over 'The Rest' at The Saffrons in Eastbourne – a game in which he had added just 15 runs and one wicket to his tally. Over the course of 24 matches during the season, Fender had scored 1,114 runs at 39.78 and taken 143 wickets at 19.49.

25th SEPTEMBER 1923

Exactly a year after he first managed the feat, Fender again completed a season having scored 1,000 runs and taken 100 wickets. Fender had just skippered Lord Cowdray's XI to a drawn match against 'The Rest' at the Central Ground in Hastings, adding no runs and three wickets to his aggregate. On this occasion, in 27 matches he scored 1,136 runs at 31.55 and took 140 wickets at 18.56.

25th SEPTEMBER 2004

The West Indies staged a dramatic fightback to beat England in the final of the ICC Champions Trophy at The Oval. Chasing 218 to win after Marcus Trescothick had scored a century for England, the West Indies were 147/8 when Shivnarine Chanderpaul was dismissed by Paul Collingwood. However, wicketkeeper Courtney Browne and fast bowler Ian Bradshaw knew they had time on their side and, over the course of 15 overs, put on 71 to wrest the title away from the hosts and back to the Caribbean.

26th SEPTEMBER 1961

Alfred Jeacocke died in Ladywell, Lewisham. Jeacocke had made his Surrey debut in 1920 and scored 5,608 runs for the club at 29.51. However, shortly after he hit his career best 201* in 1922, Jeacocke was involved in a controversy about his eligibility to play for the club. He had been born in Islington, outside of the catchment for Surrey but had qualified to play through living in the county for two years. However, Kent argued that the house he lived in with his wife was outside of the county, with Surrey actually beginning on the other side of the road. He was withdrawn from the squad for the rest of the season but returned to the side in 1923 when the rules were changed to say that any player who had qualified through birth or residency and had subsequently played three seasons for the club, as Jeacocke had, were qualified for life.

27th SEPTEMBER 2009

Graeme Smith hit his career best one-day international score of 141 against England at Centurion during a match in the ICC Champions Trophy. Despite the future Surrey captain's efforts, South Africa's 301/9 from 50 overs was not enough to win the game as England had previously posted 323/8 thanks to runs from Owais Shah and Paul Collingwood.

28th SEPTEMBER 1994

Future Surrey legend Saqlain Mushtaq made his first-class debut for Pakistan International Airlines against Pakistan National Shipping Corporation at the Ashgar Ali Shah Stadium in Karachi. He took 2-10 from 12 overs and his side won by an innings and 19 runs.

29th SEPTEMBER 2009

All-rounder Grant Elliott, fresh from an underwhelming display for Surrey in that summer's Friends Provident T20, took 4-31 as New Zealand beat England by four wickets in the ICC Champions Trophy at Johannesburg, helping them undo their previous good work against South Africa.

30th SEPTEMBER 1972

Ian James Ward was born in Plymouth, Devon. Ward made his Surrey debut against Middlesex in the County Championship in 1992 but was then released by the club and did not play again until 1996 when he appeared in a match against South Africa at The Oval, and he played three AXA Equity & Law League games that year. After playing three more times in 1997, 1998 was his breakthrough year and he never looked back, becoming a core part of Surrey's three-time championship-winning side. Ward was released by Surrey at the end of the 2003 season and played the final two years of his career for Sussex before retiring and carving out a very successful role as a Sky Sports cricket commentator. Overall, Ward played 92 first-class games for Surrey, scoring 5,738 runs at an excellent average of 40.40. In the international arena, he made his Test debut against Pakistan in May 2001 and played four more games that summer, scoring just 129 runs at 16.12 in a heavy series defeat to Australia.

30th SEPTEMBER 1972

Just over 200 miles east, The Oval was hosting its third rock concert in two years – the last to be staged at the ground. The gig was staged in conjunction with the *Melody Maker* music newspaper's Poll Awards and featured the cream of the contemporary scene in 1972, including Wishbone Ash; Emerson, Lake and Palmer (ELP) and Genesis. Tickets were £1 in advance or £1.25 on the day. Around 18,000 attended the gig and cheered as the stars of the show emerged from the Long Room on the first floor of the pavilion, where the awards were being handed out to luminaries including Rod Stewart, who was returning to the ground for the second consecutive year, having previously supported The Who with his band The Faces in 1971. Outside, crowds were kept entertained in between bands by DJ sets from the legendary John Peel.

SURREY CCC
On This Day

OCTOBER

1st OCTOBER 1863

Charles Marshall was born in Woodville, Derbyshire. A wicketkeeper, Marshall made his Surrey debut in 1893 against Nottinghamshire at Trent Bridge and represented the club until 1899, winning the County Championship three times. At the time wicketkeepers were not expected to contribute to the batting effort and Marshall played 43 times, scoring 341 runs with a best of 42. Behind the stumps he took 82 catches and made 15 stumpings.

2nd OCTOBER 1974

Matthew James Nicholson was born in St Leonards, Sydney, New South Wales. A committed fast bowler and useful lower-order batsman, Nicholson played for Surrey 21 times in 2007 and 2008. He took 55 wickets at 34.74 and also contributed 693 runs, including his first-class best – 133* – against Yorkshire at The Oval in 2008. Although he only played for the club for a short time, he was held in such great respect that he was awarded a County Cap at the end of the 2007 season. After leaving in 2008 he retired from first-class cricket, never adding to the one Test he played, against England at the Melbourne Cricket Ground in 1998.

3rd OCTOBER 2001

Widely known as a great batsman, earlier in his career Mark Ramprakash also used to boast a strong sideline in off-spin, taking 34 career wickets. One of his finest hours with the ball came during England's first one-day international against Zimbabwe at the Harare Sports Club when he out-bowled established spinner Jeremy Snape to take 3-28 from his seven overs.

4th OCTOBER 1884

Cyril Theodore Anstruther Wilkinson was born at Elvet Hill in Durham. Although Wilkinson's primary sport was hockey – winning a gold medal at the Antwerp Olympic Games in 1920 – he was also Surrey captain from 1914 to 1920. Although four years of his captaincy was wiped out by the First World War, Wilkinson made 53 appearances for Surrey, scoring 1,734 runs at 25.50 – including a best of 135. After his sporting retirement, he became a senior civil servant and was appointed a CBE in the 1954 Queen's Birthday Honours for services to hockey.

5th OCTOBER 2000

Alec Stewart and Graham Thorpe played for England against Bangladesh in an ICC Knock Out competition at the Gymkhana Club Ground in Nairobi. England comfortably advanced to the next round with Stewart hitting an unbeaten 87 to set up an eight-wicket win.

6th OCTOBER 1978

In an extraordinary coincidence, both Chris Schofield and Nayan Doshi – who jointly hold the title of Surrey's all-time leading Twenty20 wicket-taker – were born 90 miles apart from each other in Wardle, Lancashire, and Nottingham respectively. Mercurial leg-spinner Schofield joined Surrey in 2006 after a storied career that had seen him go from being one of the first centrally contracted England players to being released by Lancashire in 2004 and spending nearly two years without a professional club. During his time at Surrey he took his 53 Twenty20 wickets at 22.62 from 48 matches, also scoring 203 runs. He added a further 142 scalps and 2,338 runs in his 95 first-class and one-day games. Doshi, the son of Indian international spinner Dilip Doshi, joined Surrey in 2004 after having played in the Ranji Trophy for Saurashtra. While at Surrey he played 34 Twenty20 games, taking his 53 wickets at just 14.66. In other cricket he added another 169 wickets from 85 matches.

7th OCTOBER 2001

Alf Gover died in south London, aged 93. He enjoyed a long career with Surrey, in which the whole-hearted fast bowler took 1,437 wickets in 336 appearances as well as eight Test wickets in four games. During his career, alongside Andy Sandham and Bert Strudwick, he set up one of the most well known indoor cricket schools in England, at East Hill in Wandsworth. Gover bought out Strudwick on his retirement and later also acquired Sandham's share. He ran the school alongside his son John until 1989, with both Viv Richards and Sunil Gavaskar being coached there before going on to their incredible careers. Alongside the school Gover remained a familiar face at The Oval, standing on the committee for many years, and he was a popular appointment as president in 1980. He was born on 29th February so only enjoyed 23 'proper' birthdays but nonetheless was the oldest living Test cricketer when he died.

8th OCTOBER 1961

Alan Peach died in North End, near Newbury in Hampshire. Peach was a fine all-rounder for Surrey from his war-delayed debut against Somerset in 1919 to his final match against Leicestershire in 1931. Throughout this time he scored 8,497 runs at 23.53 and added 778 wickets at 26.04 with his right-arm medium pace. After his retirement, Peach was a Surrey coach from 1935 to 1939 and could claim significant credit for recommending the Bedser twins to the club in 1938.

9th OCTOBER 2004

Indian off-spinner Harbhajan Singh took match figures of 11-224 as India lost to Australia in the first Test at the M. Chinnaswamy Stadium in Bangalore. Harbhajan, at the time thought to be one of the most exciting young off-spinners in world cricket, joined Surrey the following summer, making his debut against Warwickshire in June.

10th OCTOBER 1959

Surrey played their first match outside England when they took on Rhodesia at the Police A Ground in what was then known as Salisbury. Former captain Stuart Surridge came out of retirement to lead a full-strength side including Edrich, Barrington, Stewart, Surridge, Loader and the Bedser twins. The first game of the tour saw a tightly-fought three-day match, eventually won by Rhodesia by just two runs.

11th OCTOBER 2007

Surrey announced that young fast bowler Stuart Meaker, a graduate of the club's Academy, had signed his first professional contract. Meaker had gained experience with the England Under-19 set-up as well as the Surrey second XI and was due to travel to Malaysia for the ICC Under-19 World Cup the following February. At the same time, Surrey also announced they had offered a new two-year deal to young Irish wicketkeeper Gary Wilson.

12th OCTOBER 2012

Surrey announced the signing of experienced left-arm spinner Gary Keedy from Lancashire. Through 215 first-class games with Lancashire, Keedy had built a reputation as one of the most reliable bowlers of his type in the domestic game.

13th OCTOBER 2001

Mark Ramprakash and Ben Hollioake played for England in the fifth one-day international against Zimbabwe in Bulawayo. England won by seven wickets with Hollioake taking 1-34 and Ramprakash scoring six.

14th OCTOBER 1914

Surrey captain and president Michael Barton was born in East Dereham, Norfolk. Barton enjoyed a good career with Oxford University before making his Surrey debut in 1948. He was appointed captain in 1949 and led the club to a joint County Championship title in 1950 before surrendering the leadership to Stuart Surridge in 1952, although he did skipper the club for a final time against Oxford University at Guildford in 1954. He served as Surrey president in 1983 and died in Sevenoaks, aged 91, in 2006.

15th OCTOBER 1989

Alec Stewart played his first game for England, a one-day international against Sri Lanka in Delhi. The game was part of the MRF World Series, otherwise known as the Nehru Cup. England won by five wickets with Stewart – playing purely as a batsman – making only four runs.

16th OCTOBER 2007

Surrey announced the signing of Pakistani pace bowler Mohammad Asif as their overseas player for the 2008 season. Coach Alan Butcher described Asif as 'one of the world's best new-ball bowlers'. Sadly, Asif never arrived at the club with his role as overseas player being rotated between Australian pace bowlers Steve Magoffin and Matt Nicholson and Indian spinner Harbhajan Singh.

17th OCTOBER 1959

Surrey started their second and final game on tour in Rhodesia, a drawn match at the Queens Sports Club in Bulawayo. Under the leadership of Alec Bedser, Surrey were dismissed for just 75 in the first innings but fought their way back into the game in the second, with John Edrich hitting 151.

18th OCTOBER 1845

Surrey CCC was formally constituted following a dinner at the Horns Tavern in Kennington.

19th OCTOBER 1989

Alec Stewart played as England recorded a morale-boosting win over Australia at the Lal Bahadur Shastri Stadium in Hyderabad. Australia hit a seemingly healthy 242/3 from their 50 overs but 124 from Wayne Larkins saw England beat the total from just 47.3 overs with 243/3. Stewart was at the crease when England won, unbeaten on four.

20th OCTOBER 1947

Younis Ahmed was born in Jullundur (now Jalandhar) in India. Ahmed made his Surrey debut in 1965 but played full-time from 1967 to 1978. He played 262 times for Surrey, winning the County Championship in 1971, and scoring 14,112 runs. Younis also played four Tests and two one-day internationals for Pakistan with a highest score of 62.

21st OCTOBER 2011

The Chicago Bears became the third National Football League side to use The Oval as a training venue. The Bears – including head coach Lovie Smith and quarterback Jay Cutler – got in the spirit of things with Cutler and star linebacker Brian Urlacher being given some rudimentary cricket coaching by Surrey's Arun Harinath and Tom Lancefield.

22nd OCTOBER 2003

Gareth Batty took his first Test wicket during England's first Test against Bangladesh at the Bangabandhu National Stadium in Dhaka. Batty had left Surrey in 2001 for Worcestershire but, in 2010, he returned to become a key player at The Oval.

23rd OCTOBER 1900

Douglas Robert Jardine was born in Malabar Hill, Bombay (now Mumbai) in India. Jardine moved to England at an early age and developed a strong reputation as a young batsman, first at Winchester College and then Oxford University. He made his debut for Surrey in 1921 and played his first Test in 1928. However, as an amateur, his business commitments began to get in the way of his cricket. Nonetheless, he was appointed England captain in 1931 and then Surrey captain in 1932. Although his style was often controversial, England lost only one match under his leadership before he retired in 1934 having captained England in the famous 'Bodyline' series of 1932/33.

23rd OCTOBER 2009

The New England Patriots, featuring superstar quarterback Tom Brady and coach Bill Belichick, became the first NFL franchise to visit The Oval when they staged a training session at the ground ahead of their match at Wembley against the Tampa Bay Buccaneers. When asked for his opinion on the ground Brady said he thought it was 'pretty cool' although he was concerned the pitch that had been drawn on to the outfield might have been measured in metres rather than yards!

24th OCTOBER 1819

Surrey's first club captain, Charles Hugh Hoare, was born in Mitcham. Hoare played in Surrey's first matches in 1846 and led the club until 1850. A member of a familial cricketing dynasty, Hoare's father played first-class cricket from 1807 to 1812, his brother Henry from 1835 to 1838 and his son – also Charles – from 1871 to 1878, including four games for Surrey. Although his achievements, 308 runs at 12.83, may seem modest, it is important to remember that at the time an average of over 20 was considered virtually unattainable. Hoare died in 1859 at Roke Abbey in Romsey, Hampshire.

GARETH BATTY, AN IMMENSELY POPULAR FIGURE AT THE CLUB IN RECENT YEARS

25th OCTOBER 1998

In his penultimate match as England one-day captain, Adam Hollioake hit an international career best 83* against South Africa in the Wills International Cup in Dhaka. Despite this his side – which also contained Alistair Brown, enjoying a rare international run – lost the match by six wickets and were eliminated from the competition.

25th OCTOBER 1929

Peter James Loader was born in Wallington. Loader was one of the key components of Surrey's incredible success in the 1950s, generating excellent pace from a body often described as 'whippet thin'. He made his Surrey debut in 1951 and played consistently until 1963 when he decided to emigrate to Australia. He played only one match for Western Australia before retiring. Loader stayed fully involved in the game though, becoming a regular umpire, a profession from which he retired in 2007. Overall he took 1,108 wickets for Surrey at 18.66 from 298 appearances. Loader died, in Perth, aged 81 in 2011.

26th OCTOBER 1961

Batting for the first time in sub-continental conditions, Ken Barrington had hit 139 for England in their first ever match in Pakistan at the Gaddafi Stadium in Lahore. Barrington's runs matched those of Javed Burki in the Pakistani first innings and helped England respond to the home side's 387 with 380. In the second innings, Pakistan subsided for just 200 and England recorded a five-wicket victory.

27th OCTOBER 2010

Richard Thompson was announced as the new chairman of Surrey CCC, replacing the long-standing incumbent David Stewart. At 43, Thompson became the youngest chairman in club history. Away from the club, Thompson is a successful entrepreneur and is also chairman of a number of other firms including M&C Saatchi Merlin, Mama Group and Debrett's People of Today.

28th OCTOBER 2006

England beat the West Indies by three wickets in an ICC Champions Trophy match at Ahmedabad. Chris Gayle and Dwayne Bravo had both hit centuries for the West Indies as they scored 272/4 but a fine innings of 90 from future Surrey man Kevin Pietersen saw England home with nine balls remaining. Another future Surrey player, seamer Jon Lewis, opened the bowling and was by far the pick of the England attack, taking 1-35 from ten overs.

29th OCTOBER 1972

The Oval staged its first game of Australian Rules Football as Carlton Football Club played a team of All Stars from other senior teams in Australia. With the middle covered by coir mats, around 9,000 people – His Royal Highness The Prince of Wales one of the few non Australian expatriates in attendance – watched Carlton win 12.12 (84) to 10.18 (78). Aussie Rules has since become a popular fixture at the ground with a further 17 games being staged.

29th OCTOBER 2010

The Denver Broncos, with quarterback Kyle Orton and coach Josh McDaniels, became the second NFL franchise to train at The Oval, ahead of their match against the San Francisco 49ers at Wembley Stadium.

29th OCTOBER 2011

Jade Dernbach and Kevin Pietersen played as England recorded a six-wicket Twenty20 victory over India at Eden Gardens, Kolkata. Dernbach took 0-26 from four overs and helped run out Mahendra Singh Dhoni while Pietersen hit 53 from 42 balls.

30th OCTOBER 2000

Alec Stewart, Graham Thorpe, Saqlain Mushtaq and Azhar Mahmood played as England lost to Pakistan by six wickets in a one-day international at Rawalpindi. Stewart hit 18 and Thorpe top scored with 39 as England were bowled out for 158, Saqlain taking 5-20 and being named Man of the Match. Neither Surrey player batted as Pakistan knocked off the required runs with more than six overs remaining.

31st OCTOBER 1942

Squadron Leader Roger Winlaw died in Caernarvon, Wales. After playing for Cambridge University, Winlaw made his Surrey debut in 1933 and played for the club for two seasons, representing them 17 times and scoring 650 runs at 30.95 before becoming captain of Bedfordshire. Already a sergeant in the RAF Volunteer Reserve, he was commissioned as a pilot officer in 1938 and called to active service at the outbreak of the Second World War. A member of No. 256 Squadron, Winlaw was piloting a plane on a training mission in North Wales when he tragically collided with another plane, piloted by Squadron Leader Claude Ashton – who had also played for Cambridge University and went on to play county cricket for Essex. Both men were killed instantly. Winlaw's widow Marsali Mary Seal de Winlaw remarried to John Montgomery three years later in 1945. The couple had a son, Hugh Massingberd, who went on to become an eminent journalist and long-standing obituaries editor of the *Daily Telegraph*. As well as many other things, Massingberd was famous for his incredible ability to retain knowledge and – a fervent Surrey fan and regular at The Oval – had a particular fascination with the careers of Surrey players Monte Lynch and Alistair Brown. After his death on Christmas Day 2007, Massingberd was honoured with a bench in his name placed outside the The Oval's pavilion. With his noted genealogical expertise, it is fair to presume that Massingberd had a very good idea about his unique family connection to the club and ground.

SURREY CCC
On This Day

NOVEMBER

1st NOVEMBER 2012

Surrey announced the signing of South African captain Graeme Smith on a three-year deal to become new club captain. Described by *The Wisden Cricketer* magazine as 'county cricket's biggest coup since Shane Warne signing for Hampshire in 2000', Smith said he was 'excited to be joining such a professional and talented team', adding that he was 'excited about what we can achieve at Surrey going forward'. Surrey's team director, Chris Adams, concluded: 'By signing a three-year deal, Graeme has demonstrated his commitment to Surrey on a long-term basis and I look forward to working alongside him and the rest of our hugely talented squad to bring more silverware to this club in the near future.'

2nd NOVEMBER 1997

A trio of Surrey players – Waqar Younis, Saqlain Mushtaq and Azhar Mahmood – played against South Africa in the Wills Quadrangular Tournament in Lahore. An extraordinary match saw Wasim Akram take three wickets in an over to keep South Africa to just 271. However, Shaun Pollock was able to repeat the trick at the start of the Pakistan innings and reduce Pakistan to 0-3 then 9-4 in his second over when he bowled Shahid Afridi. It was left to Inzamam-ul-Haq and soon-to-be Surrey star Azhar Mahmood to drag them back into it but despite Mahmood's characteristically violent 59 from 43 balls, Pakistan lost the match by nine runs.

3rd NOVEMBER 1979

Scott Alexander Newman was born in Epsom. Newman played 90 matches for Surrey from 2002–2009, scoring 6,404 runs at 42.69. The left-hander will be most remembered at Surrey for a County Championship game against Glamorgan in 2005 when he scored 117 in the first innings and 219 in the second.

3rd NOVEMBER 1996

Saqlain Mushtaq took a hat-trick in Pakistan's third one-day international of the series against Zimbabwe in Peshawar. The treble consisted of Grant Flower, John Rennie and Andy Whittall – and, with captain Alistair Campbell unable to bat through injury, ended the match – as the wily leg-spinner took 4-28 and Pakistan won by 78 runs.

4th NOVEMBER 2008

Surrey announced that Graham Thorpe had returned to the club as batting coach. Thorpe had played his last game for Surrey in August 2005 but had since then carved out a fine reputation as a batting coach at New South Wales over two seasons.

5th NOVEMBER 1962

Christopher Keith Bullen was born in Clapham. A popular off-spinner and lower-order batsman, Bullen played for Surrey 134 times from 1982 to 1989, taking 130 wickets. Since his retirement, Bullen has continued to work for the club and is now employed at grass-roots level as a cricket development manager, helping to manage the club's relationship with local clubs throughout Surrey.

6th NOVEMBER 1876

Ernest George 'Ernie' Hayes was born in Peckham. Hayes played for Surrey from 1896 until 1919, making exactly 500 appearances and scoring 25,062 runs at 33.10. Although he missed four years because of 'distinguished' service in the war that won him an MBE, Hayes is still sixth on the all-time list of players who have played the most for Surrey and also sixth on the list of all-time run scorers for the club. In the international arena he played in five Test matches but made only 86 runs at 10.75. After his retirement, Hayes chose to a run a pub – The Paxton Arms in West Norwood – until his death aged 77 in 1953.

7th NOVEMBER 2012

Some 140 years on, The Oval reunited the Wanderers and Royal Engineers for a rematch of the first ever FA Cup Final. In front of a crowd that just exceeded the 2,000 in attendance in 1872, a strong Engineers exacted their revenge, winning the match 7-1.

8th NOVEMBER 1990

Thomas John Lancefield was born in Epsom. A graduate of the Surrey Academy, the left-handed opening batsman made his Surrey debut in 2009. Sadly, injuries hampered his career and he was released at the end of the 2012 season having scored 501 runs for the club.

9th NOVEMBER 1914

An MCC committee met at Lord's and decided to award Surrey the County Championship – the club's seventh – over two months since they had played their last match of the season, a win over Gloucestershire at The Oval with Jack Hobbs scoring 141. Although Surrey had cancelled their final two games of the season due to the outbreak of war, MCC calculated the table using 'percentage of possible points gained' as the device to rank the teams. Once this had been concluded, Surrey were top with 74.4%, 4.4% ahead of their nearest rivals Middlesex.

10th NOVEMBER 2003

All-rounder Rikki Clarke played for England in a one-day international against Bangladesh in Dhaka. Clarke took 1-35 and did not bat as England won by seven wickets.

11th NOVEMBER 1916

Robert Carr, Baron Carr of Hadley, was born. Carr was elected as the Member of Parliament for Mitcham in 1950 and was an MP until 1976. He served as the Secretary of State for Employment and narrowly escaped in 1971 when members of the anarchist group The Angry Brigade exploded two bombs outside his house. He was appointed as Home Secretary in 1972 and, after Edward Heath had been defeated in a 1975 leadership election, was asked to 'take over the functions of leader'. He was created a Life Peer in 1976 and served as Surrey president in 1985.

11th NOVEMBER 1977

Benjamin Caine Hollioake was born in Melbourne, Australia. He moved to England as a young child and made his first-class debut for Surrey in 1996, three seasons after his older brother Adam. Ben went on to play 66 first-class and 106 one-day games for the club, scoring 4,235 runs and taking 225 wickets. He was a precocious talent, making his Test debut alongside his brother in 1997 having blasted 63 in a one-day international earlier in the summer. Although sometimes inconsistent, Ben was one of the most naturally talented players seen at Surrey for many years and it was a tragedy for all who knew him when he was killed in a car crash in Australia in March 2002.

12th NOVEMBER 1961

Having started the tour with a century in England's first ever match in Pakistan, Ken Barrington was 52* at the end of the first day of the first Test against India in Bombay. The second day saw Barrington go on and beat the 139 he had scored in Lahore by reaching 151. He added 52* in the second innings but India eventually hung on for the draw.

13th NOVEMBER 1848

Swainson Howden Akroyd was born in Streatham. Akroyd played 23 times for Surrey, scoring 622 runs at an average of 15.55 and was the club's seventh captain, serving in 1869 and 1870.

14th NOVEMBER 1907

Herbert Montandon Garland-Wells was born in Brockley. Garland-Wells made his Surrey debut in 1928 following a stellar career for Oxford University. He was also a talented footballer, playing for the England Amateur football team as goalkeeper. After ten years at Surrey, during which he, Freddie Brown and Errol Holmes were known as the 'Biff Bang Boys', he was appointed captain in 1939. *Wisden* later reported he led 'with a touch of unorthodoxy in the tradition of Percy Fender'. During the Second World War, he took up a career as a solicitor and was unable to return to the game afterwards. Although he stayed in England throughout the war, it is reported that his name was informally used as a code word during the North African campaign: Garland-Wells = Monty = Montgomery. As *Wisden* commented: 'This was more impenetrable to the Germans than the most complicated cipher.' Garland-Wells died, aged 85, in Brighton in 1993.

14th NOVEMBER 1971

Adam Craig Gilchrist was born in Bellingen, New South Wales. The big-hitting Australian wicket-keeper is the leading non-English run scorer in one-day internationals at The Oval.

15th NOVEMBER 1989

Future Surrey favourite Waqar Younis made his Test debut for Pakistan against India in Karachi. The young bowler took 4-80 in the first innings, his victims including Sanjay Manjrekar, Sachin Tendulkar and Kapil Dev.

16th NOVEMBER 1827

James Southerton was born in Petworth, Sussex. Southerton made his Surrey debut against his native county in 1854 and played 152 times between then and 1879, taking 995 wickets and scoring 1,665 runs. Known as one of the finest slow bowlers of the 1870s, Southerton is also the holder of a world record that is unlikely to ever be beaten – the oldest Test debutant in history. He made his Test bow in Melbourne on 15th March 1877 at the age of 49 years and 119 days.

16th NOVEMBER 2000

Graham Thorpe hit 118 for England in the drawn first Test against Pakistan in Lahore. After Nasser Hussain won the toss and chose to bat, Thorpe was 22* overnight and went on to make three figures – finding support from Craig White.

17th NOVEMBER 2011

Alistair Brown returned to Surrey as second XI coach, less than three months after finishing his professional career for Nottinghamshire. Speaking about his new appointment, Brown said: 'When I left Surrey back in 2008 I always hoped I could return if the right opportunity arose. Fortunately it has and it's very good to be back at the club I call home.' Chief executive Richard Gould uncontroversially added: 'The return of Ali Brown to Surrey is great news for both players and fans of the club. He is one of the most popular Surrey men of recent times.'

18th NOVEMBER 1995

England's first Test in South Africa for more than 30 years was rained off after a violent thunderstorm flooded the outfield at Centurion Park, causing the last three days to be abandoned. Surrey were represented in the match by Alec Stewart and Graham Thorpe, who scored six and 13 respectively.

18th NOVEMBER 2003

Rikki Clarke played for England in a one-day international against Sri Lanka at the Rangiri Dambulla International Stadium. Clarke scored two and took 0-20 as England were dismissed for 88 and lost by ten wickets.

19th NOVEMBER 1841

Henry 'Harry' Jupp was born in Dorking. Jupp made his Surrey debut in 1862 and played 252 games with his final match in 1881. During this time he made 11,452 runs at an average of 26.81 as well as taking 148 catches and making six stumpings. Jupp toured Australia with James Lilywhite's English side in 1877, playing in both Tests and scoring 68 runs. Away from cricket he was a bricklayer and pub landlord and died in Bermondsey, aged 47, in 1889.

20th NOVEMBER 2008

Surrey's head groundsman Bill Gordon was named as the ECB Groundsman of the Year for the sixth consecutive year, having shared the award in 2003 with his predecessor, Paul Brind. It was also the eighth win in nine seasons for The Oval pitch. The club's operations director at the time, Clive Stephens, said: 'Bill is the consummate professional and he and his team are thoroughly deserving of the award.'

ALISTAIR BROWN PLAYS ANOTHER CHARACTERISTICALLY ATTACKING STROKE

21st NOVEMBER 1850

George Strachan was born in Prestbury, Gloucestershire. Strachan played for Surrey for the first time in 1870 and made 54 appearances, scoring 1,186 runs and taking 118 wickets. In 1872, he was appointed captain and served until 1875. However, after handing over to Allen Chandler for a year, Strachan returned as skipper for the 1877 and 1878 seasons. W.G. Grace said of him: 'He was a good bowler and batsman: but it was by his brilliant fielding that he made his reputation; and there can be little doubt that at long-leg or cover-point he had few equals in his own time.' Strachan died aged 51, in Middleburg, Transvaal, in 1901 while in charge of the British Concentration Camps during the Boer War.

21st NOVEMBER 2006

Surrey teamed up with Fulham FC to jointly launch the ECHO Project, which aimed to help educate local children in equality, coaching and healthy options. The scheme was launched by Mark Butcher, Jonathan Batty and Fulham defender Ian Pearce at nearby Vaxuhall Primary School. The brains behind the scheme, Surrey community manager George Foster, said: 'The ECHO Project offers vital guidance on how to live a healthier life.'

22nd NOVEMBER 1998

Mark Butcher, 23* overnight, opened the innings for England against Australia in the drawn first Test at the Gabba in Brisbane. He had lost opening partner Mike Atherton the previous evening but played brilliantly against a strong Australian attack to hit 116. Later in the day, his efforts were complemented by Graham Thorpe who added a further 77 and Mark Ramprakash with 69*.

23rd NOVEMBER 1855

Walter William Read was born in Reigate. Read made his debut for Surrey in 1873 and played 366 times for the club between then and 1897, making 17,683 runs at 32.80. Known as one of the most fluid batsmen in the country, Read also played 18 Test matches, making a further 720 runs at 27.69. Read missed the infamous defeat to Australia at The Oval in 1882 but was selected to make his debut on the tour of Australia the following winter. As such, he received the timeless honour of being name-checked in the poem inscribed on the side of the urn itself, which reads: 'When Ivo goes back with the urn, the urn; Studds, Steel, Read and Tylecote return, return.' He also still holds the world record for the highest ever score from a number ten batsman in a Test, 117 against Australia at The Oval in 1884. As a Surrey player he became the first to hit a triple century for the club, 338 against Oxford University in 1888, and won the County Championship four times. He died aged 51 in 1907, having previously spent two years as a coach to young players at The Oval.

24th NOVEMBER 1894

Herbert Sutcliffe was born in Summerbridge, Harrogate, Yorkshire. Most famous for being Jack Hobbs's regular opening partner for England, Sutcliffe also holds the impressive record of being the leading Test century maker at The Oval, with five hundreds from his seven matches. His centuries came in 1926, 1929 (when he hit one in each innings), 1930 and 1931. Although he has held on to the record since his last Test in 1935, it could soon be in danger as Kevin Pietersen currently sits one behind him on the list, with four centuries from seven matches.

24th NOVEMBER 1930

Kenneth Frank Barrington was born in Reading, Berkshire. Barrington became assistant groundsman for Reading Cricket Club aged 16 and played for White Hart Hotel XI on Sundays, where he was spotted by Andy Sandham, who invited him to play for the Surrey Colts. Having made a positive impression there, Barrington was asked to join The Oval groundstaff in 1947. Sandham had since become head coach and told the young man to concentrate on his batting, rather than the leg-spinners he had previously thought his forte. After two years of National Service in Germany – during which time Barrington represented his battalion at football and won both its boxing championship and a small arms competition – he returned to Surrey and made his first-class debut in 1953. From there, he established himself and became a legend for club and country. In 362 games he scored 19,197 runs at 41.28. However, it was said that his batting improved with the quality of opposition, a statement borne out by his Test average of 58.67 and his average against Australia of 63.96. Overall, he played 82 Tests, scoring 6,806 runs. When he died of a heart attack in the West Indies aged just 50, his *Wisden* obituary simply began: 'There should be no need for reticence in anyone paying tribute to Ken Barrington.'

24th NOVEMBER 1955

Ian Terence Botham was born in Oldfield, Cheshire. The brilliant all-rounder holds the record for both the most Test wickets at The Oval – 52 – and the most Test catches – 19. His finest hour with the ball at The Oval was match figures of 10-253 in 1981 and with the bat it was his Test best total of 208 against India the following year.

25th NOVEMBER 1999

Future Surrey coach Chris Adams made his Test debut against South Africa in Johannesburg in an England side also containing Mark Butcher and Alec Stewart. It was not a day to remember for Adams who came to the crease at 2/4 and departed 50 minutes later at 34/5. Adams only made one in the second innings but 86 from Stewart and 32 from Butcher helped England to 260 all out and a loss by an innings and 21 runs.

26th NOVEMBER 2006

Popular Surrey all-rounder Graham Roope died in Grenada aged just 60, while on a charity cricket tour. Born in Hampshire, Roope nevertheless made his Surrey debut in 1964 and after making his breakthrough in 1966, never looked back, playing for Surrey until 1982. Overall, Roope played 342 times for Surrey, making 16,226 runs at 37.21 and also taking 211 wickets. He made his Test debut in India in 1973 and played in 21 Tests, averaging 30.71. He was also known for being a brilliant catcher. Away from the cricket field, Roope was a talented footballer and played in goal for several non-league sides including Corinthian Casuals, Wimbledon, Kingstonian and Woking.

27th NOVEMBER 1993

One-time Surrey spinner Anil Kumble, who played for the club 13 years later in 2006, had one of the finest days of his career when he bowled India to victory in the final of the C.A.B. Jubilee Tournament at Eden Gardens. With India defending 225/7, Kumble needed just 6.1 overs to take 6-12 and bowl the West Indies out for 123, being named Man of the Match in the process.

28th NOVEMBER 1872

Albert Baker was born in Hale, Farnham. Baker made his Surrey debut in 1900 and played regularly for the club until 1907. He played 104 matches, scoring 3,729 runs and averaging 25.89. He peaked in 1905 when he scored 1,257 runs at 31.42 with two centuries.

29th NOVEMBER 1946

Alec Bedser endured a trying first day of the Ashes at the Gabba in Brisbane. After a controversial incident when Don Bradman was reprieved when England thought they had him caught at slip on 28, he went on to dominate the day's play, reaching 162* at the close with Australia on 292/2.

KEN BARRINGTON, ONE OF THE FINEST BATSMEN IN THE WORLD THROUGHOUT THE 1960S

30th NOVEMBER 1857

Robert 'Bobby' Abel, known as 'The Guvnor', was born in Rotherhithe. One of the great Victorian batsmen, Abel scored 27,609 runs for Surrey at 36.61 and a further 744 for England at 37.20 from 1881 to 1904.

SURREY CCC
On This Day

DECEMBER

1st DECEMBER 1886

John Neville 'Jack' Crawford was born in Cane Hill, Surrey. An excellent all-rounder, Crawford made his Surrey debut against Kent in 1904 and played for the club until 1909, when a dispute with the committee meant he left for Australia where he played Shield cricket for South Australia. He made his peace with Surrey and returned to play a handful of matches in 1919. Ironically, his final game for Surrey was against Australia in 1921. In total, Crawford played 120 matches for Surrey, scoring 5,217 runs and taking 450 wickets. He twice, in 1906 and 1907, achieved the elite double of scoring 1,000 runs and taking 100 wickets in the same season. Crawford also achieved recognition on the international stage, playing for England 12 times, scoring 469 runs and taking 39 wickets.

1st DECEMBER 1901

George Lohmann died at Matjesfontein, Cape Province in South Africa. Lohmann was one of Surrey and England's finest bowlers of the late 19th century, exploiting the pitch conditions of his era to bowl deadly spin but at a medium pace. From just 292 first-class games, he took a staggering 1,841 wickets at 13.73. Sadly for Lohmann, his career was dogged by tuberculosis he contracted in 1892. From then onwards, he split his time between England and South Africa, emigrating permanently in 1897. He was last seen in England in 1901, when he managed the touring South African side, but upon his return to Cape Town, the illness he had spent most of his adult life battling became more critical and finally claimed his life, aged just 36.

2nd DECEMBER 1953

Ernie Hayes died aged 77 in West Dulwich. After a 23-year Surrey career in which he played exactly 500 times and scored 25,062 runs – as well as winning the MBE for distinguished service in the First World War – Hayes spent his last 20 years running The Paxton Arms in West Norwood.

2nd DECEMBER 2010

Kia Motors (UK) was announced as the latest title sponsor of The Oval. The five-year deal was worth £3.5m to Surrey CCC.

3rd DECEMBER 2003

Mark Butcher and Graham Thorpe played for England in the drawn first Test against Sri Lanka in Galle. Replying to the hosts' 331 all out, the Surrey pair led the way, resisting Muttiah Muralitharan as they top scored with 51 and 43 respectively in England's 235. The game ended in a thrilling draw, with Ashley Giles and Matthew Hoggard batting out the nail-biting last seven balls.

4th DECEMBER 1999

Fast bowler Sylvester Clarke died in Christ Church, Barbados, aged just 44. Having just attended the funeral of his friend, fast bowling colleague and fellow Bajan Malcolm Marshall, Clarke collapsed and died at his home just days before what would have been his 45th birthday.

5th DECEMBER 1889

Thomas Frederick 'Tom' Shepherd was born in Headington Quarry, Oxfordshire. Shepherd made his debut for Surrey in 1919 and became a regular the following summer, playing consistently until 1932. Primarily a right-handed batsman, Shepherd scored 18,254 runs at 39.68 in his 354 appearances for the club – top scoring with an unbeaten 277 against Gloucestershire at The Oval in 1927. He was also a very handy medium-pace bowler, taking 439 wickets at 30.70.

5th DECEMBER 1964

Ken Barrington, 48* overnight after M.J.K. Smith won the toss and batted in the first Test against South Africa in Durban, went on to make an unbeaten 148. Following Barrington's century and two excellent bowling displays, England won the match by an innings and 104 runs.

6th DECEMBER 1961

Having scored 139 in the first Test against Pakistan and 151* in the first Test against India, Ken Barrington continued his extraordinary run of form as he hit a century in a third consecutive Test, 172*, to ensure England drew the second match of the series in Kanpur. After conceding a lead of 223 after the first innings, Barrington partnered first with Geoff Pullar and then Ted Dexter to shepherd England to safety.

6th DECEMBER 2010

Surrey announced the signing of veteran South African all-rounder Zander de Bruyn from Somerset. An extremely accomplished county all-rounder, de Bruyn immediately slotted into the side and made a crucial contribution to the season in both 2011 and 2012.

7th DECEMBER 1990

Alec Stewart and Martin Bicknell played for England as they recorded a four-wicket win in a one-day international against New Zealand at the WACA in Perth. The game, part of the Benson & Hedges World Series, saw Bicknell take 2-36 as New Zealand were dismissed for just 158 before Stewart anchored a potentially rocky England reply with a determined 29* from 43 balls.

8th DECEMBER 2008

Former Surrey and England all-rounder Chris Lewis was arrested at Gatwick Airport after cocaine valued at £200,000 was found in his luggage as he arrived on a flight from St Lucia. Earlier in the year, Lewis had come out of retirement in a blaze of publicity to play for Surrey in Twenty20 cricket. Sadly, the experiment had ended poorly, with Lewis playing just one match and scoring only two runs. Lewis was remanded in custody and, the following year, was given a prison sentence of 13 years.

9th DECEMBER 1933

Morice Bird died in Broadstone, Dorset. Bird had attracted initial fame as a schoolboy cricketer for Harrow, hitting a century in each innings during the traditional match against Eton in 1907. Bird made his first-class debut for Lancashire that year but joined Surrey in 1909, making his debut against Oxford University. He played 127 times for the club, scoring 4,880 runs at 25.02, taking 114 wickets at 25.07 and earning the club captaincy from 1911 to 1913. Bird was also selected for ten Tests, scoring 280 runs at 18.66. Sadly his career was cut short by the onset of the First World War and he only played a small number of games afterwards, going back to Harrow as coach before picking up similar duties at The Oval. He died, sadly just 45, in Dorset having been ill for a number of years.

10th DECEMBER 1936

Bobby 'The Guvnor' Abel died in Kennington, aged 79. Abel started his career with Surrey in 1881 after learning his trade in club cricket at Southwark Park near his Rotherhithe birthplace. Abel established himself in the Surrey side in 1892 and – other than a short period in 1893 when he first experienced problems with his eyesight – was virtually an ever-present until his retirement in 1904. Abel scored 27,609 runs in 514 appearances. Although he drove and cut well, his speciality was scoring on the leg side. He overcame the handicap of being short by becoming an excellent judge of length and being very quick on his feet. In 1899, he became the third man to hit a triple century for Surrey – and his total of 357* still stands today as the highest score by a Surrey player. It was said that, after one of his many great days at The Oval, a crowd of hundreds would gather beneath the pavilion and chant 'Bob, Bob, Bob!' until 'The Guvnor' came to acknowledge his public. Abel played 13 Tests for England. He toured Australia and South Africa, scoring 744 runs at 37.20, including two centuries. In later life, eye problems that had dogged his latter career developed into full-blown blindness and he died at his home near The Oval, remembered in his *Wisden* obituary as: 'Among Surrey batsmen he ranks with Hobbs, Hayward, W. W. Read and Harry Jupp.'

11th DECEMBER 1954

Sylvester Theophilus Clarke was born in Lead Vale, Christ Church, Barbados. Clarke will be remembered by the many batsmen who had the misfortune of facing him as one of the quickest bowlers ever seen in county cricket. Surrey exploited Clarke's misfortune in reaching his peak at the same time as Michael Holding, Andy Roberts, Joel Garner, Colin Croft and Malcolm Marshall by employing him for ten seasons from 1979 to 1989. During this time he played 152 games for the club, taking 591 wickets at 18.99, and won the Walter Lawrence Trophy for scoring the quickest domestic century, exactly 100 against Glamorgan at St Helens in 1981.

11th DECEMBER 1997

Alec Stewart scored 116 for England in a seven-run one-day international win over India at Sharjah.

11th DECEMBER 2000

Surrey's Graham Thorpe gave English cricket fans one of their most triumphant and memorable moments in modern memory when he late cut Saqlain Mushtaq for four in virtual darkness to win both the third Test in Karachi and the overall series. With Nasser Hussain and Duncan Fletcher emphasising a need not to lose, England had played out a sometimes attritional series that had seemingly led to this moment. Thorpe had played his full part in the tactics, grinding out a century that contained just two boundaries during the first Test in Lahore. Finally, on the last day of the series, Pakistan snapped and lost their last seven wickets for just 87 runs. This left England 176 to win in 44 overs. However, canny to the local light conditions, Pakistan captain Moin Khan cut the over rate to its slowest possible figure. However, umpires Steve Bucknor and Mohammad Nazir played him at his own game and forced the match to continue long past the time play would normally have been called off for bad light. Thorpe was England's lynchpin, hitting 64* – one of his finest innings in an England shirt – as first Graeme Hick and then, appropriately, Hussain himself saw them home.

12th DECEMBER 1998

Mark Ramprakash, playing in the third Ashes Test at the Adelaide Oval, hit 61. Surrey's other two players in the match, Mark Butcher (6) and Alec Stewart (0), had both been dismissed earlier in the day. Stewart, also captaining and keeping wicket, redeemed himself in the second innings as he restored English pride with a pugnacious 63* despite his side slipping to a 205-run loss and Australia retaining the Ashes.

13th DECEMBER 1997

Surrey had four players in the England side that beat the West Indies by four wickets in a one-day international as part of the Akai-Singer Champions Trophy at Sharjah. The biggest contribution came from Graham Thorpe with 57 but Alistair Brown (10), Alec Stewart (23) and captain Adam Hollioake (9 and 1-41) all played their part. The victory put England into a very strong position in the quadrangular tournament as they had won both of their first two games and had only Pakistan left to face.

14th DECEMBER 1856

William St John Fremantle Brodrick, 1st Earl of Midleton, was born. St John Brodrick, as he was known at the start of his life, entered Parliament as the Conservative MP for West Surrey in 1880, moving to a seat in Guildford in 1885. By 1898 he had been promoted through a series of jobs in the Foreign and War Offices to become Secretary of State for War. After losing at the General Election of 1906 he was made an alderman of the London County Council in 1907 and became The Viscount Midleton. From 1910 onwards, Midleton – whose family had long Irish links – became deeply embroiled in Irish politics and in 1920 he was created Earl of Midleton. He was appointed president of Surrey CCC from 1923 to 1925. Further afield in his family, the Earl's brother-in-law – Sir James Whitehead – was appointed British ambassador to Austria where his daughter Agathe became the first wife of George Ludwig von Trapp. The story of their children – with von Trapp's second wife Maria von Trapp – became the basis for the musical *The Sound of Music*. Midleton's grandson Julian became Queen Elizabeth II's land agent at Sandringham and his great granddaughter Alexandra was a lady-in-waiting to Diana, Princess of Wales.

15th DECEMBER 1894

Tom Richardson took three wickets on the first day of the Ashes series at the Sydney Cricket Ground. The fast bowler went on to take two more the following day to finish with figures of 5-181 as Australia racked up 586. Despite having to follow on, England went on to win the incredibly tight match by ten runs as Albert Ward hit 117 and Yorkshire's Bobby Peel then took 6-67 as Australia were dismissed for just 166 in their second innings.

15th DECEMBER 1970

John Edrich ended the day 38* in the second Ashes Test in Perth. Edrich had hit 47 in England's first-innings 397. After Australia hit 440 all out in return, Edrich, batting with Basil D'Oliveira, was on his way to 115* in the second as England set Australia an unlikely target of 245 to win on the last day. The match was eventually drawn, with the hosts never troubled on 100/3 from 32 overs.

16th DECEMBER 1882

John Berry 'Jack' Hobbs was born in Cambridge. A batsman so fine he is known as simply 'The Master', Hobbs is for many experts the greatest player to ever play the game. On a purely statistical level his brilliance is unsurpassed. His 199 first-class hundreds are 29 more than his nearest challenger; his 61,760 runs 2,711 greater than the next man. The only reason he is not also top of Test lists is surely the far greater proliferation of the international game in modern times. For Surrey, Hobbs is simply an icon. He played for the club first in 1905 and continued for an incredible 29 seasons, simply unthinkable today. That Surrey only won the County Championship once during his career is no reflection on him, as he broke 1,000 runs in every season bar one. He holds a record for the most Surrey appearances – 598 – that will surely never be broken, despite missing four seasons in the peak of his career due to the First World War. Away from the field, Hobbs was very popular with other cricketers and had a reputation as a humorous and kind man, and 16th December is still marked by a loyal group of admirers known as the Master's Club, who honour the great man by meeting at The Oval for a lunch of roast lamb and apple pie, Hobbs's favourite.

16th DECEMBER 1910

Frederick Richard 'Freddie' Brown was born in the exotic surroundings of Lima in Peru. Brown made his debut for Surrey in 1930 and played 106 matches, scoring 3,982 runs and taking 429 wickets. A talented and aggressive all-rounder, Brown left Surrey in 1939 when he was offered the captaincy of Northamptonshire, for whom he played until 1953. Brown was also a well thought of captain of England, from 1949 to 1951 and continued to play an active role in the game until his death in 1991, aged 80.

16th DECEMBER 1961

Not content with having hit centuries in three consecutive Tests, Ken Barrington made it four when he scored 113* in England's third match of the series against India in Delhi. Sadly, the match was ruined by the weather, meaning it ended in a draw.

17th DECEMBER 1946

As if to prove that even the greatest bowlers have a bad day sometimes, Alec Bedser, playing in the second Ashes Test at the Sydney Cricket Ground, spent the day sending down the best part of 46 overs against

Australian pair Sid Barnes and Don Bradman. Both players hit 234 and Bedser's effort cost him 153 runs and – eventually – earned the wicket of Barnes. Despite receiving this punishment, Bedser later became great friends with 'The Don', with the pair regularly writing to each other and often crossing the world for visits.

18th DECEMBER 1940

Arnold 'Ob' Long was born in Cheam. An excellent wicketkeeper and effective left-handed batsman, Long made his Surrey debut in 1960 and played for the club until 1975 when he left to finish his career at Sussex. During his time at the club he took 703 catches behind the stumps and made a further 103 stumpings. Sitting behind only the great Bert Strudwick and Ted Brooks on the all-time list of wicketkeepers for the club, Long does hold the record for the most victims in a season, taking 91 during the 1962 campaign.

19th DECEMBER 2004

Mark Butcher hit 79 for England in the first Test at Port Elizabeth as they responded to South Africa's 337 in the first innings. Butcher's Surrey colleague Graham Thorpe hit just four but the roles were reversed in the second innings, Butcher getting a duck while Thorpe saw the side home with 31*.

20th DECEMBER 1954

Peter May hit the first 98 runs in a brilliant 104 that changed the course of the second Ashes Test at the Sydney Cricket Ground. After being bowled out for just 154 in the first innings and allowing Australia to make 228, May's innings – supported by Colin Cowdrey – helped England to 296 in the second innings. Needing 223 to win, 'Typhoon' Frank Tyson fired up to take 6-85 and bowl the hosts out for 184, winning the game by 38 runs and coming back to 1-1 in the series.

20th DECEMBER 1972

Geoff Arnold, in the same vein as Ken Barrington, played his first Test in sub-continental conditions and experienced immediate success. Playing India in the first match of the series at the Feroz Shah Kotla in Delhi, home skipper Ajit Wadekar won the toss and batted first. It didn't go to plan for him though, with Arnold accounting for openers Ramnath Parkar and Sunil Gavaskar as well as Wadekar and Dilip Sardesai to leave India on 43/4. They recovered to 156/7 overnight but Arnold returned the following morning to complete his Test best of 6-45 as England set up a six-wicket win.

21st DECEMBER 1925

Future Surrey president Dennis Cox was born in Bermondsey. Initially a player, he was appointed to the presidential role in 1992 and died in 2001, aged 75.

21st DECEMBER 1963

Sir Jack Hobbs died, aged 81, in Hove, Sussex. The great man had retired from cricket in 1934 and continued his already well-received career as a journalist, both in the press and in books as well as continuing to work in the Fleet Street sports shop he established using the £1,670 raised from his benefit in 1919 – which was rescheduled after his initial benefit in 1914 was deemed a failure because of public concern about the outbreak of war. During the Second World War he served in the Home Guard and – in 1946 – became the first professional cricketer to be elected on to the Surrey committee. However, due to concerns about his business and the failing health of his wife Ada, Hobbs moved his family to Hove where he began to spend more time caring for her. She died in March 1963 with Hobbs's health beginning to fail soon afterwards and he died shortly before Christmas. Two comments in *Wisden* obituary summed up his mastery. The first, from the author, said simply: 'I never saw him make a bad or a hasty stroke. Sometimes, of course, he made the wrong good stroke, technically right but applied to the wrong ball. An error of judgement, not of technique.' The second was a quote from a former opponent: 'It wer"ard work bowlin' at'im, but it wer' something you wouldn't'ave missed for nothing.'

22nd DECEMBER 1842

Richard Everard Webster, 1st Viscount Alverstone, was born in Holborn. An excellent sportsman in his youth, Webster was called to the bar in 1868 and became a QC just ten years later. He was appointed Attorney General in 1885 and became MP for Launceston the following month, exchanging his seat for the Isle of Wight later that year. He remained Attorney General until 1900, save for a brief period in 1892 and then from 1892 to 1895. He was given a peerage in 1900 and became Lord Chief Justice later that year, serving from 1900 to 1913. He presided over a number of high profile trials, including the murderer Hawley Harvery 'Dr' Crippen. He was appointed Surrey president in 1895, serving until his death, aged 72 in Cranleigh, in 1915.

23rd DECEMBER 2006

Surrey's Mark Ramprakash completed his unlikely transformation from a middle-order batsman who at one stage revelled in the nickname

'Bloodaxe' to housewives' favourite when he won the fourth series of BBC show *Strictly Come Dancing* with partner Karen Hardy. After disposing of former Spice Girl Emma Bunton in the semi-final, Ramprakash won an all-sports final over ex-England scrum-half Matt Dawson, famously receiving a perfect score of 40 for his sizzling salsa routine.

24th DECEMBER 1964

Ken Barrington completed his century against South Africa in the second Test at New Wanderers in Johannesburg. At 59* overnight, Barrington followed the example of Ted Dexter and moved on to 121. Despite England's 531, South Africa batted well and secured the draw.

24th DECEMBER 2009

Rory Hamilton-Brown returned to Surrey as captain, having originally left the club in 2007 to join Sussex. His signing was the culmination of a long – and public – pursuit by Surrey team director Chris Adams, which included visiting Hamilton-Brown in South Africa where he was training with the England Performance Programme. Adams was delighted with the signing, saying: 'To me, captains have to have certain attributes such as charisma, a galvanising spirit, intelligent and tactical brains and the ability to inspire people to follow them. Rory Hamilton-Brown has these in abundance.'

25th DECEMBER 1875

Walter Scott Lees was born in Sowerby Bridge, Yorkshire. A Surrey player from 1896 to 1911, Lees played 343 games for the club, taking 1,331 wickets at 21.44 and scoring 7,237 runs. After starting his career in the shadow of Tom Richardson, Bill Lockwood and Bill Brockwell, Lees flourished in the 1905 season, when he took 193 wickets at 18.01. He retired in 1911 and died, in West Hartlepool, in 1924.

25th DECEMBER 1975

Marcus Edward Trescothick was born in Keynsham, Somerset. Although a prolific run scorer against Surrey, averaging 40.29 in 11 matches, Trescothick holds the honour of being the all-time leading run scorer in one-day internationals at The Oval with 528 runs from ten matches.

26th DECEMBER 2004

Mark Butcher started his last Test, against South Africa at Kingsmead in Durban. Butcher managed scores of just five and 13 in the match which ended in a high-scoring draw after England's poor first innings of 139.

THE MAN SIMPLY KNOWN AS 'THE MASTER' – JACK HOBBS

27th DECEMBER 1940

Legendary umpire David Shepherd was born in Bideford, Devon. The man who is most well known for his habit of hopping when the score hits a 'Nelson' (111, 222 etc.) has umpired ten one-day internationals at The Oval, double the amount of any other official.

27th DECEMBER 1994

The great Peter May died at his home in Hampshire, just four days short of his 65th birthday. Described in *Wisden* obituary as a 'beau ideal of English batsmanship', May had an incredible career for Surrey and England from 1950 to 1963. In retirement he became an insurance broker for Lloyd's and spent time with his wife and four daughters. He was a Test selector from 1965 to 1968, president of MCC from 1980–1981 and chairman of selectors from 1982 to 1988. At the time of his death, May had never served as Surrey president so, in 1995, he was awarded the honour in absentia.

28th DECEMBER 1941

Future Surrey player and president Roger Harman was born in Hersham. Left-arm spinner Harman played for Surrey from 1961 to 1968, enjoying a stellar season in 1964 when he took 136 wickets at 21.01. However, his form never scaled such great heights again and he took just 48 in his final season. Harman stayed involved the club though and, in 2011, served a year as club president.

28th DECEMBER 1941

Intikhab Alam Khan was born in Hoshiarpur, India. Alam was a Surrey star for 13 seasons from 1969 to 1981, playing 232 games and scoring 5,707 runs. He was also a Pakistani international, playing 47 Tests and four one-day internationals and captaining his country in their inaugural one-day match against New Zealand in Christchurch in 1973. In retirement he was a successful international coach, winning the 1992 World Cup and 2009 World Twenty20 with Pakistan.

29th DECEMBER 1894

Tom Richardson took 5-57 for England in the second Ashes Test at the Melbourne Cricket Ground. On the back of a weak total of 75, Richardson was critical to England keeping Australia to just 123. With captain Andrew Stoddart hitting 173 in the second innings, England were able to set their hosts 428 to win – a target they fell 94 runs short of with Richardson taking two more wickets.

29th DECEMBER 1901

Former Surrey captain George Strachan died at Middleburg, Transvaal, South Africa. Strachan is one of two people to have led Surrey on two separate occasions, from 1872 to 1875 and from 1877 to 1878. After his retirement, Strachan served in the Boer War and was put in charge of one of the concentration camps established by British forces. He died, aged 51, at one of these camps after contracting a fever.

29th DECEMBER 1976

Saqlain Mushtaq was born in Lahore. A key figure for Surrey winning the County Championship three times in four years from 1999–2002, Saqlain played in 94 first-class matches for the club, taking 424 wickets at 21.86.

29th DECEMBER 2004

Playing alongside Mark Butcher, Graham Thorpe hit one of three centuries in England's second-innings 570/7 declared against South Africa at Durban. After 273/0 had become 314/4, Thorpe stabilised the innings by forming partnerships with Andrew Flintoff and Geraint Jones, reaching 118* before the declaration came late on the fourth day.

30th DECEMBER 1913

England completed a victory over South Africa at Old Wanderers in Johannesburg by an innings and 12 runs. The side featured three Surrey players, Jack Hobbs, Morice Bird and wicketkeeper Bert Strudwick. Of the three, Strudwick contributed most to the win, ending the match with seven dismissals, four in the first innings and three in the second.

31st DECEMBER 1929

Peter Barker Howard May – known iconically to a generation of schoolboys as P.B.H. May – was born in The Mount, Reading, Berkshire. An instinctive cricketer, May was barred from the first XI at Charterhouse School aged just 13 'for his own good' before going on to become the best schoolboy batsman in the country by far. After two years of National Service in the Navy, May went to Cambridge University and made his Surrey debut in 1950. His Test debut came the following year and he immediately stamped his class on the international game with 138 in his first innings. For the rest of his career he was a vital member of two of the most successful teams the game has ever seen – the Surrey side that won seven consecutive County Championships and the England side that did not lose a series during that same period. A natural leader, May went on to captain both sides – Surrey from 1957 to 1962 and England from 1955 to 1961. For Surrey, he played 208 matches scoring 14,168 runs at 50.41 and for England he played 66 times, scoring 4,537 at 46.77. No history of May, however brief, would be complete without a mention of his style and character. The classic Englishman, May played every shot in the book with a stylish grace that is rarely seen elsewhere. As a captain, he was a tough competitor but, to borrow phrases from his *Wisden* obituary, 'unfailingly courteous' and was 'upright in everything he did, especially the on-drive'.

31st DECEMBER 1969

The 1960s passed into the history books with Ken Barrington the decade's leading run scorer in Tests. Barrington achieved the feat despite retiring from the game in 1968 and playing his final Test at Headingley in July 1968. He scored a supreme 6,397 runs, averaging 59.79. His tally was 1,609 greater than the man in second place – Colin Cowdrey. Another Surrey player, John Edrich, was in eighth place on the elite list with 2,711 runs scored at 45.95.

31st DECEMBER 1983

Ebony-Jewel Cora-Lee Rosamond Camellia Rainford-Brent was born in Lambeth. Rainford-Brent – as well as having surely the most impressive name of any of the male or female players to have represented Surrey – is the most successful female player to have been produced by the club. Although she never played Test cricket for England, she made her international debut as a 17-year-old and went on to make 22 appearances in one-day internationals, scoring 377 runs at 23.56 and a further 20 international Twenty20 appearances, adding another 357 runs at 27.46. Initially selected as an all-rounder, two serious back injuries put her out of cricket for two years and she was advised to give up sport entirely. Playing on regardless, she fought her way back on to the international scene as a specialist batsman and was part of the dominating England squad that won the Women's World Cup, World Twenty20 and the Women's Ashes in 2009.

31st DECEMBER 1999

It seems appropriate to end the book back where it began, with Alec Stewart. Stewart celebrated the new millennium in South Africa, part of the England squad battling to a 2-1 series loss. However, the famously abstemious Stewart might have been forgiven for allowing himself a drop of the good stuff as the fireworks went up to celebrate the start of 2000. With the end of the previous decade, Stewart had matched the achievement of Ken Barrington and become the leading Test match run scorer of the decade. He did so with 6,409 runs at 40.82, narrowly beating off close challenges from Mark Waugh and Mark Taylor. Stewart's Surrey and England colleague Graham Thorpe was 17th on the list with 3,599 runs at 39.12.